# THE
# EMPATHY
# EFFECT

*Build Your Business—and Your Wealth—*
*By Putting Yourself in Other People's Shoes*

## TOM WARD
WITH GR AUBIEN

THE MAJESTIC GROUP

Published by The Majestic Group
945 Lakeview Parkway
Vernon Hills, IL 60061

Book design by Lars Söderkvist

ISBN 0-9767764-0-5

*This book is dedicated to my mom and dad, underdogs who taught me the value of empathy and gave me my foundation; and to all the underdogs of the world. Even when the odds are stacked against you, with vision, determination and empathy, you can accomplish anything.*

# *Contents*

# *Introduction*

I n the summer of 2003 it all came flooding back to me. I was in
Hawaii with the top people on my staff, rewarding them for their
great work. During our visit I went to see the movie *Seabiscuit*,
which had just been released in theaters. The true story of an underdog racehorse and the damaged but resolute people who helped
make it a winner had me crying like a baby. I immediately thought
of my late father, Jack Ward, who had been a thoroughbred buff all
his life. My dad and I shared an extraordinary bonding experience
over racehorses.

Thinking about him also made me reflect on how far I'd come.
The son of a bartender and waitress who divorced when I was five,
I had a high school education. Now I was 48 years old, CEO and
founder of two successful mortgage-related companies with offices in
five states. People were flying across the country to hear my business
advice. My dad, God bless him, was a World War II veteran who had
worked hard all his life but never owned a home. Despite my repeated
offers to help, his pride forced him to live out his years in a trailer.
Now I owned several homes in three states and had already earned all
the money I would need in my lifetime.

I thought about the long climb from my humble beginnings, and
the forces that had guided and propelled me. I remembered all the
mistakes I'd made and the lessons I'd learned.

For years I've been trying to give something back to the people
who have helped make Majestic Mortgage Corporation the leader in

its market. My purpose for the company, besides giving customers a great experience and the best possible loan products and service, is also to make sure that my loyal staff prospers themselves. Our company culture is summed up in the mission statement that I wrote late one night: "To provide an experience to our customers and our employees that is second to none."

Majestic Mortgage has never advertised. We've pulled ahead of the pack by understanding our customers' needs and giving them better service and a more pleasant experience than they could find elsewhere. Particularly in today's world, where rising affluence meets declining standards of service and civility, a large segment of the market will not only reward excellent customer service with repeat business and referrals—they'll also happily pay a little extra for it. Most people have received enough rotten service elsewhere to appreciate the difference. The idea may sound simple, but excellent customer service is very difficult to provide, and even harder to sustain over time. It requires the right business philosophy, culture and infrastructure—all of which I will describe in this book.

But the single biggest factor that has brought me to this point in my life and career, and to this Hawaiian retreat with my great team, can be summed up in one word: *Empathy*. Empathy improves relationships, whether with a family member, friend or customer. The ability to put yourself in other people's shoes, to imagine how they would feel or what would motivate them in a given situation, is an extremely valuable resource that can benefit every part of your life.

Empathy minimizes conflict and promotes prosperity. In business, it creates a better experience for everyone involved—customers, employees and management. Empathetic products and services solve problems and make people's lives easier. Empathetic management creates a more positive, productive work environment. When empathy has been expressed, the results are easy to recognize: There's better communication and a clearer understanding between the parties involved, encouraging a mutual respect. Customers feel taken care of. Employees feel appreciated and become more loyal and efficient, strengthening the company and making it more profitable. Empathy improves every situation it touches, setting off a chain reaction of positive events in a self-perpetuating circle that I call *The Empathy Effect.*

One thing should be made clear: Having empathy doesn't mean being soft or a pushover. Empathy is the less emotional cousin of sympathy. It's about understanding people's pain, motivations and points of view, not about feeling sorry for them.

With its undercurrents of compassion, The Empathy Effect might seem at odds with the cold pursuit of business profit. And to be sure, empathy can't happen without sincerity. It has to be real. But the fact is, companies that provide empathetic products and services stand the best chance of sustaining market share and profitability over the long term. The Empathy Effect is about anticipating and fulfilling other people's needs, for your mutual benefit.

A few years ago, I hung up my reins as a loan officer, entrusting the day-to-day operations of Majestic Mortgage Corporation to Kevin McGovern, the company's president and a longtime top producer. With my time freed, I launched Majestic Consulting & Marketing, a company that helps other businesses become more profitable by adopting empathetic principles. Strangely enough, in my new role I found myself consulting my own mortgage company, as well as many others. Feeling I had lots of ideas to share, I started contributing articles on consumer and management advice to newspapers and magazines, including the *Chicago Tribune,* the *Chicago Sun-Times,* *Mortgage Originator* and *Mortgage Broker;* and giving interviews to radio and TV stations. I began traveling the country presenting speeches and seminars on empathy and profitability. It seemed only natural that the next step would be to write a book.

Sitting there in the theater, I was moved by how close Seabiscuit's owner had come to giving up on the horse and its jockey—and what a shame it would have been if he had. The movie made me think about how empathy ties together with the other basic ingredients of success, like determination and perseverance, hard work and responsibility—traditional American values that my parents, like many of their generation, impressed upon me throughout my childhood.

I remember the first day of my paper route. I was nine years old, excited about delivering the old *Chicago American* in our neighborhood on the city's Northwest Side. But I was so small that when I filled the basket on the handlebars of my bike with rolled-up papers and tried to ride down the sidewalk, the whole thing tipped over and my cargo came tumbling out. My mother helped me fill it back up, and then pushed me on my way. The customers paid a dime apiece for their newspapers. I made a dollar to deliver them, and some S&H Green Stamps.

Sometimes I was shorted a paper. Returning to our side of the block I'd realize that I didn't have a copy for Mrs. Wantuck. The first time it happened I didn't know what to do, so I raced home to tell my mother.

"These people need their newspapers!" she told me without any pity. "You made a commitment here, this is your job, don't sloth off!"

Her words struck fear into me—the fear of not fulfilling my obligations. Whenever I was shorted a paper, I would spend a dime of my own money to buy a copy from a sidewalk vending box. I'd roll up the paper, slap a rubber band around it and toss the day's news onto Mrs. Wantuck's front stoop. I was making a dollar and paying back a dime to make sure I delivered what I had promised. It was my job, and I took it to heart at nine years old. I didn't realize it at the time, but by forcing me to think about Mrs. Wantuck's needs, my mother had given me my first lesson in The Empathy Effect.

I don't believe that a strong work ethic is something that's programmed into a person's DNA. It has to be taught by example. My parents gave me the message loud and clear, and they both worked their butts off.

My parents co-owned a bar with my grandmother, which she had bought with money from a settlement after a car accident. The little tavern sat across the street from a hospital on Montrose Avenue. My mom was a waitress there until she split up from my dad. The bar was not a healthy environment, with all the smoking, drinking and gambling, and God knows what else going on there.

Their divorce was ugly. It was a pretty screwed up situation for me. This was the late 1950s, and back then a kid was tainted when his parents got divorced. Later on I remember bringing notes to school and being afraid that my mom would sign with her new, re-married name. There wasn't any hyphenation back then. My dad was the second of my mom's three husbands, and she had one child with each of the three.

My dad eventually lost the bar. But he wound up serving drinks at a premier watering hole at O'Hare Airport, back in the 1970s hey-day of corporate travel and expense accounts. The divorce agreement granted him custody of me every Sunday. He never failed to pick me up. My dad made sure to find a job that left him free on Sundays, even if it meant working an extra shift at another bar on Saturday to make up for the lost income. I knew it was important for him to see me. I don't think we ever missed a Chicago Blackhawks hockey game when the team was playing at home on a Sunday. I also saw my dad on major holidays and for two weeks every summer. He always came through with his child-support payments, too: I was the courier for the $25 he paid my mother every week.

I think my dad was hoping to reunite with my mom, so it sur-prised us both when she remarried with another man a few years later. She wanted to give me some stability, I suppose. Frank, the man she married, was an electrician who owned a business. My mom and I moved from the small apartment at Sunnyside and Artesian where we'd lived with my dad, and into Frank's house around Mon-trose and Central.

The situation was a little rocky at first. There was some tension. But luckily for me, Frank turned out to be a great guy. And he did restore some stability to our lives. My mom and Frank had a daughter together, my sister Diane.

At Steinmetz High School I was into sports, big time. I played baseball and basketball. Baseball was my favorite. I always thought I could play professionally someday. My dad would have liked that, too. During my junior year our team was just one out away from hav-ing the chance to play another high school at Comiskey Park, home of the Chicago White Sox. At the time I couldn't have imagined a bigger thrill.

During the game to decide if we'll go to Comiskey, the other team comes to bat with bases loaded. Two outs, bottom of the ninth. We're up by two runs. A couple of my friends are playing the outfield. The batter hits a fly ball to center—they both run for it and knock into each other. The ball bounces across the grass. We lose the game. I remember walking the two miles back to our house, completely devastated.

My dad had moved to a suburb north of Chicago and I started playing hockey on the park district team there. My teammates and I were a bunch of misfits, but somehow we won the state championship. It was the thrill of my young life, and the first time I started to show leadership skills. I still have the letter our coach wrote me, praising my efforts in leading the team to victory.

Winning in sports gave me self-confidence as an adolescent. I felt sure of my talent and my ability to succeed. I had experienced firsthand what a competitive drive could do, and seen its power in action. Without that early confidence-booster, I might not have believed in myself enough to become a successful businessman later in life. We were the underdog team. No one would have thought we could win with that group of goofballs. But we did.

Around the same time, I started reading leadership books like Mickey Mantle's *The Quality of Courage* and *The Education of a Baseball Player*. No one told me to do it. I was just naturally interested. Reading books would become a major part of my self-education.

During our junior year of high school, a buddy and I landed weekend jobs cooking for Hackney's, a popular restaurant in the North Shore suburb of Glenview. My dad knew the guy who ran the kitchen. My friend and I would drive in from the city to work the four-to-midnight shift. The job paid $1.80 an hour. The manager also needed an after-hours cleanup crew, so we agreed to stay until 3:00 a.m., hosing down the greasy kitchen floors with 180-degree water. That work paid $5 per hour—nearly three times what we made cooking. My buddy and I thought we'd died and gone to heaven.

Still, my schedule was a grind. After working at the restaurant until three o'clock in the morning, I'd drive all the way back to the city, grab a few hours sleep, and then get up at seven for baseball practice the next morning. At four o'clock that afternoon I'd have to be back at the restaurant again.

During my senior year at Steinmetz, I had my first sales experience. I had left the restaurant and was selling cookware for an Ekco distributor. We sold cookware, cutlery, tableware, you name it. We would cold-call lists of high school students, their parents, young couples—anyone who might need an excellent set of cookware. The Ekco guys taught me how to sell. They had the greatest presentation I've ever seen. We'd do demonstrations for the customers, standing on the plates to show how sturdy they were. I discovered I was a natural at sales, and even earned the title of lead acquisition on the sales team. One time, I sold four cookware sets in one sit, for a total of $1,200. I was 17 years old.

But my future was far from clear. When I was in high school during the early 1970s, it wasn't a given that every young man should attend college. Maybe some of my friends were making plans to continue their educations, but I was oblivious. My parents never mentioned the idea of college, and even if I had wanted to go, even if I'd had the grades, I knew they couldn't afford to pay for it anyway. I didn't want to be a strain on their finances. My stepfather was an electrician, and he encouraged me to learn the trade myself.

By the time I graduated high school, I also realized that I wasn't a good enough baseball player to get a scholarship. I had always been strong on defense, but I lacked the hitting prowess to play at the university or professional levels. With the right coaching I might have made it.

Even if I couldn't go pro, I still had a huge desire to play baseball. Thanks to my record on the park district team, I was scouted to play for Oakton Community College in Des Plaines, another suburb north of Chicago. The coach, a former New York Yankees first-baseman named Bob Hale, asked me to play second base on the Oakton team. Of course I'd also have to attend the school. Tuition was low, so I signed up for a few classes. "Great," I thought, "I'll play baseball and get an education at the same time."

But before the season started, the coach left to take a job in another state. With my connection to the team gone, I lost my confidence and didn't even try out. I had already signed up and paid for my courses, but my primary motivation for attending the school had vanished. I didn't bother going to classes and wound up dropping out before finishing my first semester. I guess you could say I screwed the whole thing up.

Searching for some signal to direct my life, I decided to enlist in the U.S. Air Force. No one pushed me to do it. I just signed up on my own. My father was devastated, even though the Vietnam War and the draft were over. He was still afraid I'd be killed. My dad couldn't understand why I had quit the community college, which to him might as well have been Notre Dame. College was college, as far as he was concerned. I felt like an idiot for dropping out. I needed to get my act together, so I signed up for a four-year hitch.

The Air Force sent me to boot camp in San Antonio, Texas. I was 18 years old and scared to death. After six weeks of basic training I was shipped to Keesler Air Force Base in Biloxi, Mississippi, for 26 weeks of electronics training. My first tour of duty was at Tinker Air Force Base in Oklahoma City.

During my time in the service I never left the country. At one point we were on the tarmac, ready to fly to Turkey, but at the last minute the flight was cancelled and another group went in our place.

I was homesick and frustrated. After my experience on the hockey team I knew that I had leadership skills, and I was eager to use them. But the officer training program wouldn't accept me without a college education.

As it turned out, the Air Force had taken on too many recruits for the program that I had joined. When they asked for volunteers to get out early, I found myself at the crossroads. The only stipulation for leaving was that I'd have to join the National Guard and double my hitch. I had two-and-a-half years left on my four-year Air Force tour, so I went back to Chicago and signed up for a five-year hitch with the Illinois Air National Guard, one weekend a month and two weeks during the summer.

The Air Force taught me a trade, and more important, it gave me the discipline that I had been lacking. I was anxious to take the skills I'd learned in the Air Force and try them out in the real world. Without that chance to return to the Chicago area, I probably would have been a lifer.

I had met a woman in Oklahoma City and she came to Chicago with me. We were married in a small civil ceremony with a justice of the peace. Physically and otherwise, I was right back where I had started, and just about rudderless. I knew electronics wasn't the right field for me, but I got a job sitting on a bench testing CB radios. Soon afterwards I moved to another electronics company that wanted to hire veterans, and I started climbing the ladder.

Meanwhile, I decided to give community college another try. The Air Force had granted me an honorary discharge with full V.A. benefits, including tuition reimbursement. I enrolled in courses on sales and business at another community college. Since I was on active duty for the Illinois Air National Guard, the state paid my tuition, plus I was receiving money from the feds through the V.A. I was making $17 an hour to attend college at night. The incentive to pursue a degree could hardly have been greater. But once again, I failed to stick with it. Over a couple of years I took a handful of courses that I chose myself, never following a set curriculum. Maybe it was because I was married and had a full-time job, with a baby on the way, but soon I abandoned the idea of college entirely. We were too young and the marriage didn't work out, but it brought my beloved daughter Tracy into this world.

After dropping out of college, I found that my education was taking other forms, through my work and life experiences. A friend at another electronics company had earned a real estate license and was selling homes on the side. He urged me to do the same. "C'mon, Tom," he said. "It's just part-time. You make $700 per deal. You'd be great at this!"

His words rang true to me. It wasn't the first time that someone had encouraged my knack for sales. I thought I could make some money at it.

Still working full-time at the electronics company, I started selling real estate nights and weekends. The small company was located in the far-north suburb of Antioch. My mentor there was a guy named Bernie Wysocki. Before long Bernie left to start his own business, and the owner needed someone to manage the office. It was time for me to shift gears. I left the electronics company and started managing the real estate office full-time. I was 22 years old and had no experience running an office. But I felt confident of my leadership skills. I only had to manage a few part-time sales people—how hard could it be? I would earn commissions selling homes, plus the owner gave me a small salary and a company car. For me at that age, having a company car was the greatest thing in the world.

Peddling cookware had been one thing, but selling homes took me to a whole new level. For the first time I really tasted the thrill of the kill. I felt like a captain, leading my team into battle. It was fun.

A common characteristic among successful people, in business and in life, is their ability to recognize and seize opportunities. I think it's especially important for young people to aggressively pursue early opportunities that build a foundation for their lives and careers. Luckily, we're all bolder when we're young.

Pumped up from selling homes and managing the real estate office, I jumped at the chance to upgrade to a franchise. I got a job at a Red Carpet office, and then at Century 21. The owner paid me $125 a week to manage the office of ten people, plus I earned commissions for selling homes. The economy was in recession. Jimmy Carter was president. American hostages were being held in Iran. Interest rates were sky high, with prime at 21%. Rates on home loans had soared above 17%—out of range for many buyers.

The national mood was down, but we tried to stay upbeat. In the small town of Antioch, Illinois, which at the time had a population of 6,000, our team of 10 salespeople managed to sell a house a day for 180 straight days. We were the only real estate brokers with "SOLD" on our signs, and customers started coming from miles around. At the time I might have chalked it all up to our competitive drive. We sure felt like a winning team. But looking back I see that our success really came from The Empathy Effect.

"When somebody needs a new house," I told myself, "they will eventually buy one, even if the country is in a recession. Why not give them something other real estate agents don't offer, so they'll buy one of our listings?"

If we were selling a house similar to others for sale in the same neighborhood, how could we persuade the buyer to choose ours? We had to offer empathy. What kinds of issues were the buyers facing? What were their frustrations, their fears? We knew that most people couldn't qualify for a home loan at 17%—and they wouldn't be able to afford the monthly payment anyway. It was a nightmare when you did the math.

Then as now, I knew that people buy a house for two reasons: emotional and economic. At least back then, most buyers were willing to compromise on the emotional part. "The carpeting in this house isn't the greatest, but I know it's still the right thing to buy a house." I thought people should have the opportunity to become homeowners even if their finances weren't in great shape. With interest rates climbing, housing prices were falling. There was nothing to be gained by renting. I told my sales staff, "How can we make something happen for these people, and for ourselves? C'mon, let's get motivated here!"

Our solution was to position the seller's house as the one providing the best financial benefit to the buyer. We focused on making homes affordable, and found creative ways to finance lower-interest loans. In some cases the buyer could assume the seller's existing mortgage, which years earlier had been locked in at a lower interest rate. At 17%, new money was too expensive, but people could afford a monthly payment at 13.5%. At the same time, the seller's property became more valuable than an otherwise-comparable house down the block. We would tell sellers, "When the terms of your mortgage have made it assumable by a new buyer, then your house will actually be in higher demand in today's market." Our words were music to the sellers' ears, and buyers naturally went for the houses with the lower rates. By putting ourselves in the customers' shoes, we found a way to provide both the seller and the buyer with more value.

Eventually the sales streak ended, but I realized I had made a boatload of cash for the owner of that Century 21 office. It was time to venture out on my own. I wasn't sure if I wanted the headaches of running a business, and thought maybe I should just focus on being a salesperson. I went on some job interviews.

At the time, I wondered if the owner of the Century 21 office had taken advantage by paying me only $125 per week to run his entire company. Now I realize that the answer is definitely no, he did not take advantage of me. Running the office was part of my education. The owner gave me my first start in business and I didn't have to use any of my own money to do it. I wasn't just earning a wage; I was learning how to run a company—managing the sales force, writing checks, testing different approaches to sales and management. I could learn from my mistakes without any risk. I should have been paying him!

When I told the owner I was leaving, he said, "Why don't you buy my other office in Mundelein? I'll give you a great deal."

Opportunity was knocking, loud and clear. I borrowed $10,000 from my stepfather at 14% interest, offered a small amount of stock to my friend and co-worker Jan Kosatka, and bought the Century 21 office for $4,000 down and $6,000 over five years. I worked my tail off and paid back the loan in one year.

The Mundelein location was 30 minutes away from my old real estate market in Antioch, and because of the distance I found it difficult to service my former clientele from that area. I soon opened a second Century 21 office, this one in Lake Villa, a northern Illinois town that was closer to my old territory. We did well, and eventually I bought a third office in the town of Libertyville, a market I was eager to crack. It no longer made sense to continue running the office in nearby Mundelein, so I sold that location to a woman who had been working for me.

Friends ask me now if I was aware of being on an upward trajectory in my career, but at the time I didn't even think about it. I was just running and gunning, trying to win.

We hustled to provide good service to our real estate clients, but I could see that the buyers were getting lousy service from their mortgage companies. And it was reflecting badly on my business. I would refer a homebuyer customer to mortgage people I knew, and they would screw the whole thing up. Closings were being blown, which meant the buyer didn't get his house, the seller didn't sell, and I didn't receive my commission. To obtain a mortgage license back then, you only needed to fog a mirror (be breathing) and have $25,000 of net worth. I decided to open my own mortgage company, just so I could provide good service and a smooth closing to my realty customers. I would give them a positive experience and make some money for myself, too.

At the time that I opened the mortgage company, I had never taken a loan application before in my life. Some people thought I was nuts to jump into the business. But I soon discovered that just as we had distinguished our real estate company by solving the customers' problems, we could now use that same empathetic approach to set the mortgage company apart from its competition. Though I wasn't cognizant of it yet, I was already practicing The Empathy Effect. Unconsciously I knew that empathizing with the customer was the right thing to do, even if I didn't know the reason why. Being empathetic was second nature to me then, and had started with the early lessons my parents taught me—making sure Mrs. Wantuck got her newspaper. "You have to take care of these people."

My mother's words carried more weight than she ever knew. Her message stayed with me even as she slipped away from us.

I had been lucky enough to remarry with the greatest woman in the world, the love of my life, my wife Renee. I knew myself better now, what I was and what I wanted, and she provided the stable family life that I had never known. After all those fractured years before I met her, Renee showed me what a tightly knit family was supposed to look like. Not only did she give our family a happy home, but she was also a producing real estate agent and managed one of our Century 21 offices. The birth of our first daughter, Jaclyn, brought balance and purpose to our lives. Renee's parents moved back from retirement in Florida to be closer to Jackie, their first grandchild. It was great to see how she rejuvenated their lives. My father-in-law, Bill, would end up starting a small business here, and his wife Monica provided daycare. In fact, I think Jackie turned out as smart and healthy as she is because of the great daycare her grandmother provided. Jackie added years to the lives of Renee's parents. They lived near us, and Jackie gave them something to look forward to. Her name, Jaclyn, pays tribute to my late father Jack, and to my older sister Lynne, who had died in a car accident in 1989, at the age of 47.

In 1992, Renee was pregnant with our second child. At the same time, my mother entered the hospital for surgery on an aneurysm—and she never came out. She lingered in intensive care for a month and then died.

My mom had a hard life. She was always a big smoker. My dad too, until a scare with tuberculosis in his 30s made him kick the habit. And there was all the drinking in that bar. My mom was tough as nails, but she finally found herself in a situation she couldn't escape. Not long after moving from the city to live closer to us, she checked into a hospital for what was supposed to be a routine operation. But there were complications—blood clots formed throughout her body. The doctors had to amputate one of her legs. My mom was a quality-of-life person. She wouldn't have wanted to be on a machine, in a home, without a leg. And here she was an amputee on dialysis and hooked to every machine you could imagine, communicating only with smiles and small hand gestures. Finally everyone in the family agreed it was time to disconnect the wires. We put her into hospice and she passed from there.

The weirdest part was, while my mom was dying, my daughter Nicole was being born—*in the same hospital*. I went to see my mother during every one of the 31 days she was under care. I developed a routine: I knew where to park and used the hospital's back entrance. I remember visiting my mom in intensive care on the third floor, and then going downstairs to see my wife in the maternity ward. Life was being given, and life was being taken away.

Just as an opportunity can suddenly appear, fate provides other signs at crucial moments. The day before our daughter Nicole was born, I rushed Renee to the hospital for what would turn out to be false labor. Meanwhile, my mom was dying upstairs. I was pretty whacked out by everything that was happening. Ed Conarchy, a close friend and one of my top loan officers at the mortgage company, urged me to blow off some steam by taking in a couple of races at the track. A horse that we owned together with my dad was running that day. At first I said no, I wasn't going to see the horse run.

"C'mon, Tom," Eddie said. "It will do you some good." He talked me into going, and our horse won the race.

Afterwards, while Eddie and I were driving back, Renee's water broke. She delivered the baby at two o'clock the next morning. We had pretty much decided to name her Nikki. By 4:00 a.m., I was drained and decided to head home from the hospital and get some sleep.

For some reason I took a different route home that night, maybe because I was so tired. I hadn't eaten, so I was starved, too. I stopped at a convenience store to buy some donuts. I wanted the freshly made kind, but it was so early in the morning that they hadn't even been delivered yet. So I bought a box of packaged ones instead, and a Diet Coke. Completely exhausted, I handed the cashier a $20 bill. She gave me back my change: two singles, a five and a ten. I shoved the wad of bills into my pocket and drove home, wolfing down the donuts along the way.

Later, when I awoke at 11:00 that morning, I pulled on the same pair of jeans I'd been wearing the night before. I was about to leave for the hospital when I checked my pockets and found the bills. And I could not believe what I saw: On one of the singles, someone had written "NICOLE C." in red crayon, in huge letters across the face of the bill.

I felt a chill go through me. At the hospital I told Renee, "You're not going to believe this—I know we talked about the name Nikki, but we've got to name the baby Nicole. And her middle name has to start with a C!"

Our youngest daughter's name is Nicole Courtlyn Ward. To this day I'm amazed by the bizarre randomness of being given that particular bill. What were the chances? The timing had to be perfect: If I had driven my usual route home, I would not have received the bill. If I hadn't paid with a $20, I would not have received the bill. If I had paid with three singles, shown up five minutes later, if Renee had really gone into labor the night before, I would not have received the dollar bill with our daughter's name written across it in a child's red crayon letters. I wondered about the person who'd written on the note. Did a kid give it to another kid? Did an adult rob a child's piggy bank to go buy coffee at a convenience store in the middle of the night? Who knows?

Just as I had with my mom, I received some signs just before my father died. By the mid 1990s, I had sold the Century 21 offices to concentrate on running Majestic Mortgage Corporation. Business was doing well. Having made a conscious decision to provide customers with empathetic service and a great overall experience, in an industry notorious for its bad service and shady operators, we had carved a market niche and were thriving on referrals. My dad, meanwhile, was past 70 and still tending bar. But he still seemed strong and healthy. I thought he had years left ahead of him.

Sitting there watching *Seabiscuit* in Hawaii, those days all came rushing back to me. Besides telling the story of an underdog winner, the movie is also about loss and the profound influence of father-son relationships. My dad loved the track. It wasn't about gambling. He was never a big gambler. He was an aficionado of thoroughbred racehorses.

Toward the end of my father's life, I was blessed with the opportunity to do something extraordinary for him. The mortgage company was having a good year, so I bought my dad a thoroughbred racehorse. I've never seen anyone so happy. It was unbelievable. I had been driving to a Chicago Bears football game when I got the call on my cell phone that the filly was available. Her name was B Royal Lady, which was odd because my mother's name was Bernice, and everyone called her Bea. The trainer was a friend of ours named Terrell. The horse had been in training and Terrell helped us find her.

To our amazement, B Royal Lady won her first race. My dad and I went crazy with excitement, like a couple of kids. Watching the horse win and then going down into the winner's circle for photographs with her was the biggest adrenalin rush I'd ever experienced. Terrell was a big guy from Arkansas, standing about six-three, 250 pounds. He came over and threw his arms around us. "I want to let you know somethin'," he drawled. "With some guys, I have to get them seven horses before they have their first win. Other times, the horse has to race seven times before the first win. You sons of bitches have had your horse only seven days, and you've already had your first win!"

With some other investors we rounded up more money and bought a few more horses. There was lots of overhead: food and veterinary bills, boarding and training fees. The horses had to be winners just to cover their expenses, let alone make a profit for the owners.

By then Renee's parents had moved back to the Chicago area. My father-in-law, Bill, was a retired union truck driver who had also done some bartending. I suggested he start a small courier business, with my company, Majestic Mortgage, as his first customer. At the time Bill was already in his 70s, with emphysema, and on oxygen. But the next thing we knew, his little courier operation was thriving. He picked up other customers and started pulling in $40,000 a year. My dad, meanwhile, had been serving drinks for nearly half a century, and he was ready to give up the grind. I said to him, "Dad, why don't you do some part-time courier work with Bill?" He agreed.

My dad had been working with Bill for a couple of years when one morning, during his first stop of the day delivering documents in the suburbs, he died of a heart attack behind the wheel. Even as his life was slipping away from him, my father was more worried about others than about himself. He had the intestinal fortitude to slow down the car and not let it damage anyone else's property. When it finally came to a stop against a tree, the car had been moving so slowly that there was no visible damage to either the car or the tree.

It was only by chance that my dad and I got to spend his last afternoon together, taking in a few races at Arlington Park. Renee and I had been on vacation with our daughters at the family condominium on Amelia Island in Florida. We were scheduled to fly home on a Saturday afternoon, but by Wednesday I was feeling antsy to get back. At the time I couldn't have said why—it was just some nagging feeling that I'd better return to the office. Something might be wrong, I thought. I called the airline to see if I could fly back a couple of days early. There was a flight available, so I grabbed it. I would pick up Renee and the girls at the airport on Saturday.

I got back to the office on Thursday morning and started doing some work. It was raining outside. That afternoon I got a call from my dad.

"Let's go to the track. See if Eddie wants to go, too."

The three of us had been there together so many times before that the other regulars thought Eddie and I were brothers.

"Dad, it's raining out," I told him. "You know I don't go to the track in the rain."

"C'mon, it's not too bad. Let's go." He talked me into it. Eddie and I drove out to meet him at the track. Rain was still falling, and sure enough, the track was sloppy with mud. During one of the races we could hear the sound of an ambulance siren wailing on the road behind the backstretch, but trees blocked it from our view.

"Well, that son of a bitch is dead," my dad said.

I thought it was an odd thing to say, and I looked at him. But I didn't reply.

Afterwards in the parking lot, my dad walked to his car and Eddie and I walked to mine. He had forgotten to give me something—I don't even remember what it was, binoculars or maybe a newspaper article. Turning a corner in the parking lot I saw what would be my last image of him, through water and windshield wipers, standing there in the gray rain holding something in his hand. As always, he was wearing his silver diamond ring.

The next morning a chaplain called from Northwest Community Hospital, asking me to come there. "Something has happened with your father."

And that was it. He was gone.

Just as with the "NICOLE C." dollar bill, I was amazed by the randomness of what transpired with my dad and me. If I hadn't felt that strange compulsion to fly home early from Florida, I would not have shared my dad's last day with him. And I ordinarily never went to the track in the rain.

It was almost as though my dad's life had been waiting to cap itself off with the experience of owning a thoroughbred—and a winner, to boot—before it could end. At his wake, we displayed pictures of 19 wins with our horses.

After he died I lost the thoroughbred fever. It wasn't the same without him. My dad was a fun guy, and it had been great to watch him act like a kid when his horse won, even though he was 70 years old. Ever since he died, I've been wearing his ring on a chain around my neck.

What was the lesson in this experience? That the same empathy and work ethic my parents had instilled in me as a kid also allowed me to improve their lives at the end? That's probably a big part of it. But the experience also taught me the importance of following hunches and grabbing opportunities, avoiding the "coulda-woulda-shoulda" syndrome. What if I had never bought that horse for my dad, when I had the opportunity? How bad would I have felt if I'd missed that chance?

Hunches, dreams, vision and empathy all flow from the same source. They're about intuition and imagination, and having a finely tuned radar for the signals you're receiving.

For me, the advice in this book was learned the hard way, through years of mistakes, trial and error, books and seminars, ups and downs, a brush with bankruptcy—and finally, success and financial reward. My business happens to have been housing and mortgages, but The Empathy Effect is essential for anyone who serves a customer. The principles I describe all come back to empathy. Like spokes of a wheel, they're dependent on each other and stronger as a whole, turning in the self-perpetuating circle of The Empathy Effect.

# Chapter One

# *The Empathy Revolution*

L ittle by little, The Empathy Effect has the power to change the world. If the most successful companies are the ones that offer empathy, then this planet becomes a better place. Of course, empathetic improvement isn't limited to companies—it also works for individuals, groups, organizations, even nations and international alliances. In the business world, The Empathy Effect gives people better products and service, less stress, and more civil and courteous interactions with one another. If negativity is a debit, taking something away, then empathy is a deposit in the bank, an investment that grows and pays dividends.

At its most basic level, empathy means understanding pain. If you've never experienced pain yourself, then you won't empathize with the pain of others. Of course there are many different levels of pain—it might be something life-altering and profound, like losing a loved one, or as mundane as receiving shoddy customer service. Major or minor, pain or the anticipation of pain in another person is what triggers The Empathy Effect. When you show customers that you understand what they're feeling, and you take steps to improve their experiences, you will win their loyalty. That's also how The Empathy Effect grows referrals. Whether you're offering convenience, reliability or luxury, a product or service that creates The Empathy Effect should give the customer a better experience than they'd find elsewhere. Such unique selling propositions are based on empathy, so I call them "empathy-based USPs."

## Empathy in Bermuda Shorts

Especially in industries where competition is intense, consumers will naturally gravitate toward companies that show them empathy. Take the airline business, for instance. As the industry continues to struggle through its prolonged slump, why has Southwest Airlines managed to soar above the rest, posting profits for 52 consecutive quarters (as of the first quarter of 2004), while other airlines have suffered major losses? Economies of scale, no-frills, point-to-point routes and independently unionized pilots are big parts of the Southwest equation, but the fundamental reason for the airline's success is that it shows empathy to its customers and employees. And Southwest's employees demonstrate empathy for each other. Known for USPs like low fares, reliability and a fun experience, the Dallas, Texas-based company states its mission as "dedication to the highest quality of customer service, delivered with a sense of warmth, friendliness, individual pride, and company spirit."

As part of their training, Southwest's pilots load bags onto airplanes, so they'll understand what the luggage handlers face every day. After having the experience firsthand themselves, the pilots gain an appreciation for the difficulty of the baggage handlers' jobs. Even the famously charismatic Herb Kelleher, who became Southwest's CEO in 1982 and practiced an open-door policy for all levels of the company's employees, was himself known to load passengers' bags on holidays. For their part, the baggage handlers spend time riding in the cockpits with the pilots, so they'll understand the pressures and responsibilities of flying commercial aircraft.

By helping the pilots and baggage handlers better understand one another's jobs and stress factors, Southwest Airlines' training program practices The Empathy Effect. The results are easy to recognize: There's better communication and a clearer understanding between the parties, which encourages teamwork and mutual respect. Labor relations are notoriously strained within the airline industry, and labor costs remain one of its biggest barriers to profitability. But Southwest has maintained greater harmony between labor and management while also consistently turning a profit. Not coincidentally, pilots have received bonuses based on the airline's profitability, and all Southwest employees have had the option to buy stock in the company.

Fostering a stronger understanding between its internal departments also helps Southwest Airlines create a better experience for its customers. The company has earned a reputation with the public for minimal delays and hassles. Much of the credit for that reliability belongs to the empathetic infrastructure that keeps things running smoothly at Southwest Airlines.

Since Southwest only flies 737s, everything is interchangeable—from parts to pilots. Every Southwest pilot knows how to fly every Southwest airplane, so there's never a problem switching between routes. Airlines that fly a variety of airplane models have to maintain an inventory of replacement parts for all of them, and employ different levels of pilots specifically trained to fly the various aircraft. When substitutions are needed, backups are slim and take time to find. Southwest's consistency with its pilots and planes is a money-saving economy of scale that helps keep airfares lower, and it also improves the customer's experience by minimizing delays caused by mechanical or crew issues. Because of the short runs, fun atmosphere and low airfares, passengers don't mind that there are no assigned seats and they only get a bag of peanuts to eat during the flight. Southwest also pioneered the e-ticket concept as a money-saving innovation, a brilliant move considering that paperless ticketing actually improves the customer's experience. The company's counter personnel are flexible and versatile, and can substitute as flight attendants on short notice.

I remember waiting to board a Southwest flight in San Diego, when I overheard the counter girl talking to her boyfriend on the telephone:

"Honey, why don't you just go to the gym tonight, because I've got to pinch-hit here. I know I was supposed to be home in half an hour, but one of the flight attendants got stuck in traffic and she's running late, so they need me to fly to Tucson."

The counter people and flight attendants all dress the same, in polo shirts and Bermuda shorts, making transitions between the departments that much easier. Southwest's culture is upbeat and friendly, and the company only hires people who fit that vision. The organization understands what frustrates people about air travel, and goes out of its way to avoid inconveniences for its customers—providing a positive experience at a reasonable price. That's The Empathy Effect. Southwest has earned the airline industry's top consumer-satisfaction record, according to statistics compiled by the U.S. Department of Transportation. Employees also benefit from The Empathy Effect at Southwest Airlines, which has been rated by *Fortune* magazine as the best company to work for in the United States.

## E-M-P-A-T-H-Y, M-O-U-S-E

Regardless of the product or service that you sell, from airplane tickets to movie tickets, practicing The Empathy Effect means understanding what makes your customers tick. Few entrepreneurs have empathized with consumers like Walt Disney did. Along with being a master showman, the founder of the Disney companies was one of America's top practitioners of The Empathy Effect. A high school dropout with incredible emotional intelligence, he created a vast entertainment empire through his keen insight into human nature. Disney understood what his audiences wanted and how to deliver it. More than that, he knew how to touch people. He appealed to our emotions without pandering. Whether the product was movies, television shows, cartoons, comic strips or theme parks, Disney reached the child inside of everyone. He provided a perfect example of how empathy ties to vision and dreams—the intuitive ability to imagine something before it exists. On a more practical level, Disney built an infrastructure to fulfill the wants and needs of his customers.

At Disneyland in California and later at Walt Disney World in Florida, he demonstrated an uncanny foresight for what the customers—and the kids—would enjoy. He had the vision and the guts to tell himself, "I think people will like this, and I'm going to go ahead and build it for them."

Disney's fantasy theme-park formula was so successful, and attracted such huge crowds, that the company's next challenge became figuring out how to keep the lines moving. With massive numbers of people arriving daily at the parks, even the perception of stagnant lines for the rides could have dampened the Disney magic. Who wants to pay top dollar to stand in long lines in the hot sun? What fun would that be, especially for excited, energetic children? Part of the genius of the Disney theme parks is that the company realized customers wouldn't be put off by long lines if they could see that the lines were moving. Disney pioneered a progressive, snaking system, so that as each person advances at the front of the line, the entire queue moves up behind him. Better yet, the Disney Company installed video monitors over the lines to entertain people with movies and cartoons, and created shade so they wouldn't have to stand in the hot sun. At Disneyland in California, the long line for the Indiana Jones Adventure actually becomes fun, as customers trek through a series of themed chambers on their way to the ride.

Quick-moving lines are just one of Disney's many empathy-based USPs, along with the emotional connection audiences feel to its make-believe characters, and the joy the company has given to generations of its audiences. Walt Disney felt empathy for his customers, and in return they made his vision a beloved household name.

## Building an Empathy Empire

A newer company that's enjoyed remarkable growth by demonstrating empathy for kids and their parents is Build-A-Bear Workshop. Founded by retail veteran Maxine Clark, the St. Louis, Missouri-based chain lets kids create their own teddy bears as a birthday party activity. Like many companies that offer empathy-based USPs, Build-A-Bear Workshop is all about the experience. Parties are held inside the stores, and each child custom-makes his or her own teddy bear in a fun, entertaining and interactive process. Kids choose the color, texture and softness of their bears: "Do you want your bear stuffed hard, or do you prefer it cuddlier? What kind of eyes do you want on your bear?" Kids also pick out the bear's clothes, and kiss its heart before it goes inside.

Clark, who had climbed the ladder for 25 years at The May Department Stores Company and then served as president of Payless ShoeSource before launching Build-A-Bear Workshop in 1997, credits her success to having insight into the desires of the American consumer. She shows empathy for the children, appealing to their emotional needs and creativity; and to the parents, who are grateful to find a low-stress birthday party format that their kids will enjoy. Build-A-Bear Workshop has been such a smash hit, in fact, that the chain has grown to include more than 150 locations in the United States and Canada. The company's empathetic approach to children's retailing is also spreading around the globe, with new stores opening in the United Kingdom, Japan, South Korea and Denmark.

On the Build-A-Bear website, the company's explanation of its marketing philosophy provides an object lesson in The Empathy Effect: "For so long, businesses were faulted for showing emotion," it says. "They were considered unprofessional and inappropriate. But at Build-A-Bear Workshop, we believe that is how you build a successful company—one passionate, emotionally attached person at a time."

## Get Yer Empathy Motor Runnin'!

Building a following of passionate, emotionally attached customers isn't just a successful formula for children—it also works with middle-aged adults. The approach has fueled the incredible rise of Harley-Davidson, another company that's garnered huge market share by showing empathy for its customers.

Similar to Starbucks, Harley-Davidson sells an experience that makes its customers feel good about themselves. The company understands the angst of aging Baby Boomers, and has built its USPs around alleviating some of that distress. Harley-Davidson practices The Empathy Effect by providing the sense of release and freedom craved by people who feel caged-in by their lives and careers. Even a buttoned-down, corporate accountant can cut loose and be an Easy Riding rebel on the weekends, as he roars down some country highway on his Harley.

And just as Starbucks creates a feeling of community among its loyal customers, Harley-Davidson also provides a sense of belonging through its Harley Owners Group (H.O.G.). "Express Yourself in the Company of Others," the tagline reads. "The Harley Owners Group is more than 800,000 people around the world united by a common passion: making the Harley-Davidson dream a way of life."

The great motorcycles and empathy that Harley-Davidson offers its customers have translated into mammoth world market share and profitability for the company. Harley-Davidson, Inc., announced record revenue of $1.17 billion for the first quarter of 2004. That's the profit power of The Empathy Effect, cranked full throttle.

## People Happily Pay for Empathy

A friend of mine told me about a great experience he had with a company's empathy-based USPs. Valentine's Day was coming up, and he noticed that his pregnant wife could use some new slippers. "The soles on her old pair were worn thin, and they couldn't have been very comfortable on our hardwood floors," he said.

He had a couple of choices: He could go downtown and find a pair in a department store for about $20, or he could order some pricey slippers from a gift catalog he'd received unsolicited in the mail from RedEnvelope. The catalog showed a pair of fluffy white slippers with interlocking red hearts on top. They had extra-thick soles and were supposed to be very comfortable, "like walking on a cushion of air," according to the catalog.

The only problem was the price. RedEnvelope's slippers cost about $40, and with gift wrapping and shipping, my friend would be out $50—more than twice what he'd pay downtown. But then he started thinking about the experience of shopping downtown versus shopping online. Chicago was having a nasty winter, with snow and sub-zero wind chills. Traffic was terrible, and parking would cost $20. That left taking taxis, for about the same price; or the bus, which would cost only $2 but take an hour and a half.

Then there was the experience he could expect in the department store: fighting crowds, sweating in layers of winter clothes, standing in lines, receiving indifferent service from the surly clerks. He also thought about the product itself: The heart slippers were only available from the catalog company. The department store brands probably wouldn't be as comfortable or well made, or have the red hearts for Valentine's Day. "My wife likes romantic stuff," he said. "I knew the heart slippers would be a hit."

So he ordered the $50 slippers online, fully aware that he was paying more than double what department stores charge for their slippers. But he felt the premium he paid was well worth it—for the quality of the product, and for the hassles he would avoid. And thanks to RedEnvelope's empathy-based USPs, the customer had a great experience. The website was appealing and easy to use. Immediately afterwards an email confirmed his order, and the next day another one came saying that the product had been shipped. It arrived in two days. Inside the cardboard shipping box there was a red gift box, tied with a silky, ivory-colored ribbon, and a personalized gift card. For $50, my friend received more value from the catalog company than he would have for $20 at a department store. RedEnvelope knew how to improve his experience, because it understood the consumer's situation. And the company communicated that empathy before the sale, by clearly showing its USPs on the catalog cover—along with the promise to make sure that "every little thing is just right," with the customer's gift order. People who've had a great experience with any company will soak up that empathy and radiate it back. My friend will do business with RedEnvelope again, and he won't mind when they send him promotional catalogs and emails. And here he was telling me about the company, recommending the experience.

If you have the empathy to give your customers a great experience, you will be rewarded with repeat business and referrals—which are what any company needs to sustain profitability over long periods of time. As your empathetic reputation spreads, you set a standard for other companies to follow. Step by step, The Empathy Effect can change the world.

# Chapter Two

# *What a Difference a Little Empathy Makes!*

The Empathy Effect becomes especially valuable in places where you don't expect to find it. Take the present state of health-care, for instance. In an era when insurance companies dictate the treatments a patient can receive, and doctors live in fear of malpractice lawsuits, the image of empathetic practitioners like Marcus Welby, M.D., making house calls has become a quaint relic of the past. In today's litigious, "managed care" environment, the old-fashioned notion of a soothing bedside manner has also vanished from most doctors, along with the personal care that they used to give their patients. Like shoppers at big-box retail stores, most patients nowadays are shuffled through examination rooms with minimal attention. You're lucky if the doctor even remembers your name, let alone your personal medical history.

Not long ago, I was pleasantly surprised to find an exception to this rule of indifferent, modern-day medicine. I had gone to a clinic where I was diagnosed with an upper-respiratory infection. They prescribed antibiotics and sent me home.

But the drugs didn't work. A week later I was still really sick, missing work and worrying my family. So I went back to the clinic.

They had me take a few deep breaths from an oxygen mask, and gave me a chest x-ray. It turned out that I had pneumonia. "Do you have a regular doctor?" the clinic people asked, knowing they could no longer treat me at that stage.

"Well, yeah, I have a medical group that I've gone to before, but to be honest, I'm not very fond of them."

"In that case, we highly recommend a doctor named David Drexler."

What the heck, I thought, I'll give this guy a try. And the minute I made the phone call, I could feel The Empathy Effect starting to come from Dr. Drexler. He agreed to see me right away—and when you're sick, that's what you need, not to set an appointment for a week from Thursday. Right off the bat, it appeared that I had found a doctor who showed empathy for his patients. And not coincidentally, he'd come highly recommended. The empathy wheel was turning.

When I arrived at Dr. Drexler's office for my appointment, I only had to wait a few minutes. The first thing he did was take me into a room with a couple of easy chairs, where he gave me a consultation. Immediately I could tell that he was no ordinary doctor.

"We're going to do the examination here shortly," he said, "but first I want to spend about 30 minutes explaining my philosophy to you, how I do things and how I'm different from other doctors, so you'll know what to expect and where I'm coming from. My first promise to all of my patients is that you will never sit in my waiting room for more than 10 minutes."

I was very impressed. I thought to myself, "This doctor really has a revolutionary approach." Better yet, under his care I started feeling better within days, and pretty soon my infection was gone.

Amid the double whammy of rising medical costs and declining standards of patient care, Dr. Drexler stood out by showing empathy for his patients. As always, The Empathy Effect is self-perpetuating and circular: Dr. Drexler shows empathy for his patients, and in return they give him loyalty and referrals. Since my first visit, I've referred him at least 30 times. The clinic has probably referred him many more times than that.

Because Dr. Drexler spends more time with each patient, he can't see as many patients as other doctors can. Is that the right thing for him to do, from a businessman's perspective, especially since Medicare and insurance companies limit what he can charge for his services?

Will Dr. Drexler's lower capacities ultimately hurt his business?

I realized that the answer was no. Because he's creating The Empathy Effect, over time Dr. Drexler's practice will grow and thrive. He'll retain his patients instead of losing them, and they'll refer new ones, improving Drexler's long-term profitability and his ability to sleep at night. I'm convinced that part of the reason he takes his more involved approach is simply because he's a great human being. I will probably keep going back to Dr. Drexler for the rest of my life. Compare that sense of loyalty to the indifference I had felt for the medical group I went to before—I wasn't impressed, so I won't be back. They'll constantly be looking for new patients to replace the ones who don't return. Ironically, healthcare organizations that try to increase profits with impersonal care wind up losing patients, while doctors like Drexler who provide The Empathy Effect with individual, compassionate attention are the ones who profit most.

## Rise or Fall, It Depends on Empathy

If the idea seems too idealistic that companies practicing The Empathy Effect will be the most successful, consider all the businesses that have failed by not practicing it. The difference becomes especially stark when you contrast companies within the same industry that have risen or fallen by providing or withholding empathy.

In the airline industry, Southwest has filled a market niche for short, budget-priced flights. But what about the major carriers that fly longer domestic and international routes? It could be argued that some foreign carriers—Singapore Airlines, Virgin Atlantic, KLM—have more empathy and take better care of their customers than their American counterparts do. But even when looking exclusively at U.S. carriers, clear differences emerge on the basis of empathy.

Compare American Airlines and United Airlines. American developed a highly effective, empathy-based USP by figuring out what bothered people most about air travel: cramped seats. In response, the company tore out rows in economy class and created more legroom for everyone. Branding and advertising soon followed, and before long

American became known as the airline with more legroom. Especially for tall people with long legs, the extra space between the rows is a huge draw. In another example of the reciprocal nature of The Empathy Effect, American Airlines has shown that it's listening and cares about the needs of its customers, who in turn appreciate and reward the gesture by choosing American over the more cramped competition. American Airlines is the number-one carrier in the United States.

Meanwhile, the number-two carrier, United Airlines, continued to disregard the comfort of its passengers, cramming them into economy class with their knees pressed against the backs of the seats in front of them. And lo and behold, United has filed for Chapter 11 bankruptcy protection. To be fair, lots of other factors have been dragging down the profitability of major air carriers (high labor and fuel costs, the huge expense of maintaining regional hubs, a drop in business and leisure travel after September 11, and even passengers' fear of the SARS virus). American Airlines has dipped close to bankruptcy itself. But all else being equal, consumers will naturally prefer companies that demonstrate an understanding for their needs. In the first quarter of 2004, American Airlines posted an operating profit of $42 million, while United announced a net loss of $459 million. The Empathy Effect fosters gratitude, repeat business and referrals, while indifference—or even downright antipathy—creates resentment and alienates customers.

Comparisons on the basis of empathy can also be drawn between Federal Express and the U.S. Postal Service. When it comes to overnight shipping, FedEx has raced past the post office not only in terms of delivering packages, but also by delivering what people actually want and need. When the Postal Service first tried to crack the market for overnight package deliveries, its tagline was, "Guaranteed Overnight Delivery, Or Your Money Back." People might have assumed that the policy was mostly academic, but next thing they knew, customers had to request refunds because their packages weren't reaching their destinations overnight. The heart of the Postal Service failure lay in the fact that it didn't seem to know what mattered most to its customers. The Postal Service demonstrated a lack of empathy, making it vulnerable to the competitive threat of a new company that would take the trouble to find out what consumers wanted, and then provide it.

FedEx knew that when people send a package for overnight delivery, they don't want a refund—they want the package to reach its destination overnight. The company's slogan, "When It Absolutely, Positively Has To Be There Overnight," summed up the empathy-based USP that has made FedEx the top contender in its field.

## The Aggravation Effect

To see how a lack of empathy can bring down an entire industry, look no further than telemarketing. Never has a business suffered more by demonstrating a blatant disrespect for the American consumer. Of course, the telemarketers' customers were the companies selling products or collecting research—not the hapless people whose dinners were interrupted by the annoying calls. Just as empathy is rewarded, a lack of it is punished. Sure enough, the American public eventually brought about the demise of the telemarketing industry, by pressuring Congress to create the National Do-Not-Call Registry.

The downfall of telemarketing leaves a void for all the companies whose need for product sales and consumer research created the industry in the first place. Now we're seeing the emergence of permission marketing, the process that author Seth Godin describes in his book of the same name, whereby companies like Pottery Barn and Victoria's Secret use the more empathetic alternatives of catalogs and emails to stay in touch with past or prospective customers. Still, a big gap remains in the wake of the telemarketing industry's plunge under the waves of public tolerance—and it's just waiting to be filled by some innovative new company that can devise a more empathetic means to sell products and gather research.

## What Good Is a Timeshare If You Can't Use It?

Sometimes a newcomer arrives with an empathetic improvement on the flawed original. When the idea of timeshare vacation properties was first introduced, it seemed like a good one: People who wanted to invest in a vacation home but couldn't afford to own one outright could still buy a share in such a property, along with a pool of other buyers. A house on the beach in Florida, for example, could have its ownership divided amongst multiple owners who would each visit it at different weeks of the year. Instead of spending $300,000 on an oceanfront property, you could buy 1/52nd of it, for $5,800.

While the concept might have sounded promising at first, it didn't take long for people to recognize the flaws inherent to the timeshare model. The share that each individual investor purchased would typically allow them to use the property during only one, set week of the year—the first or the second week, the 10th or the 20th week, etc. Year after year, you could only use the property during that particular week.

But what if your circumstances change as the years go by, and you can no longer visit the vacation house during your assigned week? Maybe you have kids and now they're in school at that time of year, or your new job makes it impossible to get away during that particular week. Timeshares were doomed by a failure to appreciate the customers' need for flexibility—by a lack of empathy.

Seizing an opportunity to make the flawed original obsolete, Marriott Vacation Club devised brilliant, empathy-based USPs that would revolutionize the timeshare industry. People still buy timeshares, but with the key difference that now they can swap with other owners for different weeks of the year, and even for different resort locations around the world. It's easy to imagine the collective reaction of timeshare owners: "Now, that's more like it!" Marriott's Vacation Club concept appeals to a variety of human needs—flexibility and freedom, pride of ownership, and the desire for a legacy to pass down through family generations. By recognizing and catering to these needs, Marriott has demonstrated The Empathy Effect in droves.

## When the Bubble Burst, Only Empathy Survived

Maybe there were lots of reasons why so many Internet-based companies disappeared when the dot-com bubble burst in the late

1990s (like the nagging necessity to make a profit, for one), but it's clear that the online survivors are those that practice empathy for their customers.

Look at Amazon.com and eBay. When the ruins of failed e-commerce ventures were smoldering in the distance behind them, these innovators carried on by devising and delivering empathy-based USPs. Not only do Amazon.com and eBay provide products and services that consumers actually want, but they deliver them with ease and convenience, always striving to improve the customer's experience. Amazon.com has evolved beyond selling books to now act as a broker between buyers and an extensive list of vendors selling everything from frying pans to electric guitars. Even as the scope of its offerings continues to expand, Amazon.com still finds new ways to improve the customer's experience for its old standbys of books, movies and music. The website learns the tastes of its individual customers, and in a process called data mining, its makes recommendations based on patterns demonstrated by past purchases. If you bought the DVD of *Casablanca*, maybe you'd also be interested in *Lawrence of Arabia* or *Doctor Zhivago*. The Amazon site also offers a "one-click" purchase option, so consumers who have already registered can buy products with incredible ease. These empathy-based USPs save people time and help build market share for the company.

## "Finally, Somebody Got It Right"

EBay is also an e-commerce innovator that's thrived by providing The Empathy Effect for its customers. The original premise of eBay's online auction service was akin to a garage sale on the Internet, but now it has evolved into a vast international market for the buying and selling of goods—from trinkets and jewelry to shrink-wrapped pallets of brand-new vacuum cleaners. As one friend put it, "This is exactly how the Internet should work: simple, smooth and seamless." The online marketplace is reliable and easy to use, and always operates with the convenience and needs of its customers in mind.

This friend, who lives in New York City, had bought a new computer for his home. The computer came with a printer, and a full rebate for the price of the printer. "In other words, the printer was free. And I didn't need it, because I already had one."

After the printer arrived, it was taking up space on the floor of his apartment. "I didn't even open the box."

So he decided to try selling it online. "I'd never used eBay before, but I thought I'd give it a shot."

As a first-time user, he went to the website and filled out a few quick forms, and then read a simple tutorial explaining how the eBay process works. It even showed how to use some basic HTML strokes to spruce up the advertisement for his printer that would appear on eBay, with eye-catching type fonts in different colors. He used a digital camera to photograph his printer—the box had graphics on the outside—and then uploaded the image to his ad on the eBay site. Interested buyers could start with a minimum bid of $50, or choose the "buy now" option and get the printer for a set price of $100, plus shipping and handling. As the seller, my friend set both prices himself. Before posting his ad, he weighed his printer on a bathroom scale and entered the number into the eBay site, which automatically calculated the cost of shipping and handling for the buyer.

"Since this was my first time, it took me about 45 minutes to learn how to use the system, and another ten minutes to publish my ad."

He left home to run a few errands in Manhattan. When he re-turned two hours later, his fiancée was home and he wanted to show her his ad on eBay.

"Instead, much to my amazement, I found an email saying that the printer had already been sold. I couldn't believe it."

As just one of the online powerhouse's many empathy-based USPs, eBay's PayPal service has alleviated customers' concerns about the reliability of its buyers and sellers. Buyers can pay for their eBay purchases with a credit card, even if the seller is a private citizen. The seller receives credit through his or her PayPal account, and then can choose to be sent a check, pay another bill with the money, or use the credit to make a purchase from eBay. Operating like a credit report, the system also rates the history of the buyers and sellers, based on their past eBay transactions, to verify the reliability of both parties. This way, the seller is assured he'll be paid, and the buyer knows she'll receive her merchandise.

"I accepted the bid and the money, chose UPS for the shipping, and then clicked 'yes' to print out a pre-paid UPS mailing label, with all of the necessary codes."

He wrapped the box in craft paper, taped the UPS label onto it, and then dropped off the package at a UPS Store two blocks from his apartment. Next thing my friend knew, there was $114 in his PayPal account. He later used the money to make a credit-card payment.

"The entire process was smooth and easy, with a very strong WOW factor," he said. "I thought to myself, 'Finally, here's an Internet company that's got it right.' There were no gaps, no way for some part of the process to get screwed up. Everything was taken care of."

This friend's experience with eBay showed The Empathy Effect in action. The company understood and anticipated all of the customer's needs, and then fulfilled them without missing a beat. In return, this first-time user would become an eBay booster, talking up his experience and referring it to all of his friends.

## Discovering The Empathy Effect

When a company practices The Empathy Effect, everybody wins. The customers have a great experience, the entire organization prospers, and employees are happy and loyal.

But before 1995, the year I made the conscious decision to re-brand Majestic Mortgage with empathy-based USPs, the company was just another name in a crowded, price-based industry. Even today, mortgages are often viewed as a commodity product, with price as the only distinguishing factor. People think mortgage companies are a dime a dozen. Homebuyers look for the lender with the lowest interest rates and fees.

The problem is, in this bargain-basement environment, standards of service are virtually nonexistent. The attitude towards customers seems to be, "I promised you a low rate, but I never said I'd return your calls." After filling out a loan application and getting an approval, the customer hears nothing for weeks. Then at the last minute, the mortgage company finally calls, asking for some vital document and sending the customer into a mad scramble. The closing could be blown.

As a rookie to the business, I was amazed that such lax standards could be widespread in an industry that serves the largest, most important purchase most people will ever make: buying a home. Conventional wisdom said consumers were willing to accept crummy service from mortgage lenders in exchange for the lowest possible interest rates and closing fees. No one seemed to question this status quo—not the consumer, and definitely not the people selling the loans. It didn't make sense to me.

After muddling along in the business for eight years, I still couldn't figure out how to make money with price. Because in reality, no one ever has the lowest price. The guy across the street can always go lower. More important on a personal level, operating a bargain-basement business just didn't feel right to me. My conscience wouldn't let me take a customer's money and then give them indifferent service. The whole idea ran contrary to everything I'd always believed and been taught. I couldn't go around dropping off rate sheets in a lame attempt to lure customers. It seemed crazy.

Just as everybody wins with empathy, with the bargain-basement mentality, somebody has to lose. A corner has to be cut somewhere. I wasn't going to short the customer, so I'd end up shorting myself instead. Just as I had spent my own dime for Mrs. Wantuck's paper as a kid, now I was sacrificing my company's profit for the sake of the customers.

I lacked a clear direction for the business. The Internet was just starting to take off, and everyone was buzzing with the idea that online applications were going to make traditional mortgage offices obsolete. The reduced overhead would let Internet lenders offer lower rates and fees—so consumers would naturally choose cyber-mortgage companies over the bricks-and-mortar competition. But like many assumptions in the business, this one didn't ring true to me.

"Look at these online applications," I would say to my staff, shaking my head as we looked at the competition's websites. "They ask the customer to check a box indicating whether they want an adjustable-rate mortgage or a fixed-rate mortgage. How should the consumer know which option is best for them? They need a human being to explain the difference!"

Already feeling that homebuyers deserved better service, I read a book that would give me the push I needed to re-brand my company. At a seminar for mortgage professionals, speaker Todd Duncan recommended *The Discipline of Market Leaders: Choose Your Customers, Narrow Your Focus, Dominate Your Market*, by Michael Treacy and Fred Wiersema. This book was a revelation to me. The authors argue that to become dominant, a company should market itself according to one of three "value disciplines"—low price and minimal hassles, like Wal-Mart and McDonald's; product innovation, like Intel and Nike; or "customer intimacy," where companies like Nordstrom and Airborne Express make a concerted effort to know their customers, and then create products and services based on the customers' needs. Which of the disciplines you choose depends on the particular value that your company offers. Market leaders, Treacy and Wiersema wrote, have the discipline to choose one of the three paths—and not flinch when they lose business to customers who prefer the others.

Of the three value disciplines, "customer intimacy" immediately hit home with me. I would get to know my customers and give them what they wanted and needed. As I turned this idea over in my mind, I soon realized that the concept of understanding your customers is rooted in empathy. It means seeing things from their point of view. These had been my values all along—but caught in the mainstream of the price-based mortgage business, I had lost sight of what was really important to me. Now I was able to define my own values more clearly and consciously. I would create an Empathy Effect for my customers, and my attentiveness to their needs and preferences would naturally be rewarded. "This is who I am," I told myself. "This is what I've got to be."

# "Backwards Thinking," and the Profit Power of Empathy

When I made the decision to re-brand Majestic Mortgage, I knew that empathy for the consumer would be the key to our transformation. To offer value that was unavailable elsewhere, I had to understand the customers, to put myself in their shoes. Our USPs had to solve the customers' problems.

Figuring out our empathy-based USPs required what I call "backwards thinking." Instead of offering something for sale and hoping people would want to buy it, we went the other way, to the back of the issue. We thought about what the consumer wanted and needed, and then created USPs to fill those demands. It's what author Rick Kash describes in his book *The New Law of Demand and Supply*: Find out what people want, and then supply it. What I discovered was that most consumers will tell you what they want, if you ask them.

I came right to the point: "What do you hate about the mortgage business?" People were frank with their answers. "I hate the fact that I gave the loan officer my paycheck stub, and then someone else from the company called me a week later and said, 'Mrs. Smith, I'm still waiting for your paycheck stub.'"

I decided that one of our key, empathy-based USPs would be a promise not to pester customers for documents. We would never give people the "Colombo" treatment: *"Just one more thing…. Just one more thing…."* We would gather all of the customer's documents at the beginning, submit the application, and then approve the loan file quickly.

We were empathetic enough to understand how stressful closings can be for homebuyers. Most mortgage companies don't prepare customers for this momentous transaction. Having received price-based service, the homebuyer isn't told until the last minute the size of the check he'll have to present at the closing. Often the final amount is far larger than the customer expected, and at the 11th hour they're sent rushing for a cashiers check. The customer's deal to purchase the new house might not close, and meanwhile they've already closed on the sale of their former house that morning. All of the family's possessions are stacked in moving vans. If the closing is blown, where will they move to?

To provide the value of a more positive customer experience, we devised the empathy-based USPs of accurate figures for the customer three business days before the closing, and a rehearsal of the transaction. Now the customer would know exactly what to expect, with no last-minute surprises. It just made sense. The customers would welcome the improved experience, and then recommend us to their friends. We also created a Move-Up Tax Analysis that shows people the tax advantages of upgrading to a larger home. Customers appreciate this empathy-based USP because they realize that without it, they probably wouldn't have understood the tax implications that could be the deciding factor in whether or not they buy their dream home.

When a drop in mortgage-interest rates sparked the refinancing craze, we created an email Daily Market Report and Mortgage Trend Index, to keep customers informed while they wait for rates to reach their targeted levels. The Daily Market Report summarizes how financial news affects the movement of mortgage-interest rates. Like the Dow Jones Industrial Average for mortgage rates, the Mortgage Trend Index pools rates and fees from top lenders across the country to determine the day's average, which customers can track over time. An Auto Alert email feature lets them know when their target rate has been reached, so they can lock it in.

Looking at these USPs together, I realized that we were offering a consultative approach to the mortgage business. In an industry notorious for its terrible service and shady operators, we would offer exactly the opposite—The Empathy Effect. Every customer gets a personal, face-to-face consultation, where we analyze their entire financial situation, their particular circumstances and goals, and then recommend the loan product that's best for their needs. The consultation shows the customer how their home purchase fits into the big, long-term picture of their finances, and they enjoy concierge-level service.

When the customer arrives, the friendly receptionist already knows her name. "Good afternoon," she smiles. "You must be Mrs.

Smith?" She hands the customer a menu of complimentary beverages. "What can I get for you, Mrs. Smith?"

What we had begun to offer was unheard of in the mortgage business, and pretty soon the referrals and repeat business started rolling in. To this day we close about 99% of the loan applications that we take. Empathy creates profitability.

## Fishing for the Right Customers

Learning to provide The Empathy Effect means clipping the wires in your brain. Especially in a traditionally price-based industry, re-branding to premium-priced, empathy-based services requires a fundamental shift in the company's attitudes and practices. In my industry, consumers were used to hearing horror stories about loan closings. They'd come to expect a bad experience—and unfortunately, to accept it. In that price-based norm, consumers could only look for the best of the worst.

We worked hard to develop and refine our empathy-based USPs. I knew that our services offered value, but our next challenge became finding customers who would appreciate our approach, particularly in such a crowded field of price-based competitors. How would we prove ourselves?

I was reminded of that challenge years later, during the 2003 Hawaii trip with my top producers. I found myself thinking about it early one morning. And I mean *very* early: 4:30 a.m.

The guys wanted to try deep-sea fishing. Our hotel in Wailea recommended a good charter company—they had a 46-foot boat, and 23 years of experience helping novices like us catch marlin in the waters around the Hawaiian Islands.

I am not a fisherman. It's just never been my thing. I told the guys to go ahead without me.

"Oh, c'mon, Tom," they persisted. "Come with us."

So I agreed. But they didn't tell me the details. They didn't mention that whenever you go deep-sea fishing, you have to be at the boat by 4:30 a.m.

I'm on vacation in Hawaii. My family is here, too. When somebody says I have to get up at four o'clock in the morning, it just doesn't work for me. But I've made a commitment, so I drag myself down to the dock at 4:30 a.m.

It's still dark and the harbor is full of fishing boats. High masts and reels are bobbing and clanging. I meet my team at the charter boat, and they're all standing around looking groggy. The sun won't be up for another hour and a half.

The guys from the charter company help us climb into the boat. "Here are the rules of the game," one of them says. "If you're going to puke, don't do it in the boat. You've got to puke over the side."

He shows us a photograph of a 600-pound blue marlin. The boat pulls away from the dock and starts churning through the harbor. "I want to let you know something," the guide says. "For the last couple of days, the fish have not been biting."

Great. I wish I was still in bed. But there's no turning back. I can't grab a taxi to the hotel.

The captain takes us into the waters near a beautiful, crescent-shaped island off of Maui. No one else is around. "Usually it's really busy out here," he says. I figure we must be too early. One of the guides takes us to the stern to check the bait and poles. There are hundreds of lures, colored pink or blue, shaped like little squid. But will they help us catch a fish?

Guys from my company are taking turns sitting in the big chairs facing the back of the boat, with the harnesses and the holders for the heavy poles. We're out there for a while, catching nothing. The boat circles left and then right. Still nothing.

"All right," the captain says with determination in his voice. "Here's what we're going to do. It's time to try the *Blue Channel*."

I have no idea what a Blue Channel is. At this point, I don't really care. When we reach it half an hour later, eight-foot swells are rising on the ocean. The boat starts heaving up and down. Observing the captain's rules, the guy sitting next to me loses his breakfast over the side. I'm thinking, "Great. I got up at four o'clock in the morning. We've been out here for five hours. We're not going to catch any fish.

And now the guy next to me is puking over the side of the boat. And we paid $2,000 for this!"

The captain says he'll look for a buoy where the big fish gather, "But sometimes ships come through here and knock it over." He tries using a depth finder, but still can't locate any marlin. Then he starts looking for birds. "If we find the birds, then we find the marlin."

I'm thinking, "Can't we just go home?" We're six or seven miles out to sea. I can't see land anywhere.

"Now guys, you've got to be careful about catching a wahoo," the guide announces. "It looks like a piranha, with sharp teeth. If one gets into the boat, keep away from it. We'll have to hit him over the head with a baseball bat."

One of our guys snags a fish. It flies up on the line and starts flapping around on the deck. Everybody scrambles away from the fish, thinking it's a wahoo. But the guide tells us not to worry—it's just a harmless mahi-mahi. The guys start slapping high-fives and taking pictures with the fish.

Another top producer takes his turn in the chair. And five minutes later he lands a wahoo. Four feet long, spear-shaped and silver with bulging eyes and an open mouth full of sharp teeth, the fish is jumping around on the deck, snapping its jaws.

The guide steps forward with the baseball bat and whacks the wahoo over the head. But the vicious fish is still alive, flapping around looking for something to bite. The guide hits the wahoo again, pounding its head with the bat. Finally the wahoo dies. He opens its mouth to show us its rows of jagged teeth.

After what feels like 27 hours, we finally return to the harbor. The guide says it's traditional to display flags representing the fish you've caught. He hoists two flags on our mast. I'm still not convinced that we've received an experience worth our $2,000. And then I start noticing the other boats in the harbor: There must be 30 of them, and none are flying any flags. Ours is the only one. The guys have pictures with the fish, and shots of the wahoo with those awful teeth. I start to realize that this charter company, which had been recommended to us, had gone out of its way to give us a better experience than the competition could offer. We're the only ones who caught any fish, even if one of them was a wahoo. We feel proud of ourselves.

*But wait a minute*, I think to myself: What if the fish had jumped into the boat? What difference would it make who the captain was, what kind of boat he sailed or the lures he used if the fish were jumping into the boat? How good would the company have to be?

At the time, the mortgage industry was just starting to wind down from a refinancing boom that had been roaring for years. Interest rates had been at their lowest levels since the Kennedy Administration, and just about every homeowner in America had already jumped at the chance to save money by refinancing their loans. Some people refinanced several times during the boom, whenever rates fell. In this thriving market, even the worst, least empathetic mortgage companies didn't have to try very hard to attract business. Their switchboards were lighting up with calls from motivated customers. Mortgage people, many of them gold-rush newcomers looking to stake their claims from the refinance craze, were so flush with business that half the time they didn't even return their customers' calls.

What happens when fish stop jumping into the boat? Now it would be far more difficult for all the rookies to keep their doors open. Consumers would still buy homes, but winning purchase business is a lot harder than fielding calls for refinances. It requires a genuine understanding of the customer's needs, and the will and discipline to deliver a superior experience.

When fish stop jumping into the boat, what gets tested? The boat and its captain get tested. Can they withstand the choppy waters of that Blue Channel? Will their lures really snag new business? When supply starts to outstrip demand, only those players offering great customer experiences will survive. And great customer experiences start with empathy.

## Stay the Course

I believe that the market is divided into thirds: Whether you're running a premium-experience company with empathy-based USPs, or a bargain-basement operation with bad service, one third of the market will jump into your boat no matter what you do. They might never come back, but they'll at least try you once. Another third will choose your company for the particular value that you offer—your low prices or your excellent service. And the remaining third will never give you their business, because they prefer the opposite discipline.

Re-branding to premium-priced, empathy-based USPs requires the courage of your convictions. It means never looking back. I realize that now, but during our first year after re-branding, I constantly questioned my decision. It was difficult to create valuable, empathy-based USPs—and even harder not to buckle under price objections. As the owner of a company selling premium-priced, empathy-based services, you've got to accept it as normal that you will lose business based on price. It requires intestinal fortitude. When you're struggling to increase sales, it's not easy to turn away four customers in one week who all tell you that your closing costs are too high. You have to resist the temptation to make concessions for price-based customers. Ideally, you should be in a situation where you can afford to pass on business.

Switching to the empathy road didn't make my company profitable immediately. It took time for our reputation to build. In the mortgage business, we have to sell two customers for every loan—first the homebuilder or Realtor who serve as lead sources, and then the homebuyer. Our empathy-based USPs are designed to appeal to both customers, helping the lead source sell more homes, and giving the homebuyer a great experience. Before long we started to attract the third of the market that's willing to pay a small premium for empathetic service. The price difference is minimal, and a couple hundred dollars more in closing fees compared to the lowest-priced shop in town. The empathy we offer customers helps us gain market share, repeat business and referrals—the real drivers of sustained profitability, along with economies of scale on the operations side.

The Empathy Effect requires a sincere commitment from your entire organization. It can't be just a pretense. Some companies invest in illusionary touches: expensive furnishings in the reception area, wood paneling and granite finishes—all meant to convey the image of a classy, successful operation. "Wow, look at the mahogany on these walls," the customer says. "These guys must be really good!" But these illusionary trappings say nothing about the quality of service the customer will receive. Maybe the company has spent everything on its showy reception area, but neglected to build the right infrastructure and culture behind the scenes. Lo and behold, the customer ends up having a bad experience—and he won't return or refer his friends. Surface glitz might help land the first deal, but it won't bring customers back without a foundation of empathy.

My advice to any business owner who decides to take the empathy road is to stay the course. Human nature often makes people give up on a new idea before it's had a chance to bear fruit. The company winds up reverting to a price/service hybrid, which simply does not work. It has to be one or the other.

When you decide to offer your customers premium-priced, empathy-based USPs, it's okay to have doubts. It's only natural. But stand firm, because your decision will ultimately pay off in spades. I've lived it, I know. These are not uncharted waters. Stay the course.

# Chapter Three

# *Empathy and the Advice Business*

As I dug deeper into the meaning of The Empathy Effect, I realized that empathy is essential for anyone whose living depends on giving advice to customers. And the more I thought about it, the clearer it became that far more jobs revolve around giving advice to clients than it might at first appear. For starters, there are the professional services—legal, accounting, management consulting. These professions are all premised on the idea that the provider of the service has spent years studying and gaining expertise and credentials in a given discipline or specialty, and that's what makes him qualified to advise clients on matters related to their professions.

But a vast range of other businesses, services and jobs involve dispensing advice to customers—from financial planners to department-store cosmetologists. Real estate agents, public relations professionals, even doctors use their knowledge and skills not only to provide a particular product or service, but also to make recommendations to clients on the best courses of action they should take. And empathy is the key to good advice. Without it, the people involved won't connect. No one can offer meaningful recommendations—the kind that customers will appreciate and happily pay for—unless they truly understand and empathize with what their customer is experiencing. Businesses that offer customers helpful advice can charge a reasonable premium over their price-based competition, demonstrating clearly the value of The Empathy Effect.

## Talking Turkey

It's a week before Thanksgiving. A colleague and his wife are somewhat nervously preparing to host their first holiday dinner.

"We really don't know what we're doing," he says. "My wife is a great cook, and she's seen lots of Food Network shows about cooking turkeys, but she's never cooked one herself. The family is coming over, and we don't want to screw this up."

They have lots of questions—and things to buy. Besides the turkey and the trimmings, which require a long list of groceries, there's also the roasting pan, all the gadgets for cooking the turkey, the serving platter, a tablecloth. The list goes on and on. His wife has agreed to cook, but it's his job to buy everything she'll need to prepare this huge, momentous meal.

In the newspaper he notices a color insert from a local home-furnishings store, advertising roasting pans for $29.99. "It sounds like a great deal, but I wonder about the quality," he says. "I can get all the kitchen stuff we need in one stop at this store, but I know that this retailer's angle is size and selection, not service."

He hasn't ruled out the big chain's enticing low price, but decides to stop first at Chef's Catalog, a smaller store specializing in cookware and kitchen accessories. The minute he walks into the place, three ladies working there are eager to help him.

At first he shies away, figuring they're out to give him the hard sell. He says he's just looking. But the customer quickly becomes baffled by all the choices and prices in the store. They carry six different models of roasting pans, ranging in price from $39.99 to almost $200. What are the differences between them, and which pan will be best for his needs and budget? "Suddenly I realize that I really need some expert advice."

For the customer in this situation, empathetic service is more valuable than the chance to save a few bucks. One of the saleswomen asks again if he has any questions. Luckily for him, it turns out she's been cooking turkeys every Thanksgiving since before he was born.

"She ends up giving me incredibly helpful advice," he says. "She explains the differences between the pan materials, how aluminum conducts heat better than steel, and the fact that professional chefs like Emeril Lagasse prefer a regular surface to non-stick—to get a better gravy from the 'crunchy brown bits' at the bottom of the pan. She says I don't need a lid for roasting a turkey, and points out that the big pan would be harder to store." (This kind of thorough personal service, by the way, used to define Marshall Field's in Chicago before the department store's recent owners and their State Street flagship lost empathy for the consumer.)

At Chef's Catalog, the saleswoman even gives the customer advice on how to cook the turkey—"stuff that I never would have known otherwise," he says—and recommends the area's best grocers and meat markets.

In the small specialty store he winds up buying all the kitchen equipment his wife will need to prepare their first Thanksgiving meal. He pays $10 more for the roasting pan than what the big-box store was charging for its lower-priced model (which, as it turns out, really sells for $39.99, not the $29.99 advertised in the newspaper—you have to mail in a rebate form and wait a couple of months to receive the other $10), but the small premium is well worth it for the empathetic advice that he receives. The saleswoman has put herself in the customer's shoes, anticipating and relating to the challenges that she knows from her own experience he will face. Her advice will end up making the difference between a great Thanksgiving meal and a terrible one. She has earned a loyal customer who won't soon forget her great service. "Whenever we need new stuff for the kitchen," he says, "we'll know who to call."

I don't mean to suggest that smaller stores with better advice and more empathetic service are necessarily more profitable than the big-box, mega-selection competitors, which benefit from lower prices through volume buying and other economies of scale. But the Chef's Catalog example shows the difference that empathetic advice can make to a consumer. Both stores are offering their own varieties of empathy, and which one will prevail over time depends in part on the tastes and preferences of the larger buying public. But as someone running a mortgage company that has more in common with Chef's Catalog than with Linens-N-Things, I can see the strong market niche open to any player who's willing to offer empathetic service and advice.

## What's the Customer Feeling?

Even within the arena of premium-service companies, where customers know they can count on expert advice, superstars soar above the mediocre by demonstrating insight into the customer's needs and situations. In any advice-oriented business, the professionals with the most empathy will be the best. They'll earn the highest fees and have the least competition. These empathetic advisors can relate to the concerns of their target market, making them better equipped to improve people's lives, businesses and careers. It's easy to see why customers appreciate and reward empathetic service.

On the other side of the advice business, the mediocre and outright-lousy players don't understand their clients' problems or situations. How can someone give another person helpful advice when they have no idea what it's like to be in the other person's shoes? Anyone in the advice business who does not have empathy for the customer is going to be mediocre, at best—and vulnerable to being crushed by a competitor who does have empathy.

In the advice business, to create The Empathy Effect and its concentric rings of benefit, you have to know what the customer is going through. There seem to be two ways to learn about the customer's situation. One is to walk through the pain and learn it firsthand, to be a product of the same environment as the customer and know their circumstances from personal experience. Alternately, if you've never shared the customer's experiences yourself, you can still become an empathetic advice professional—and by extension, a success—by deliberately accruing knowledge about your customer's preferences.

Through reading, interviewing, observing and absorbing, you can come to understand what the client is experiencing. The key is to go beyond the dry data, past the cold facts and figures, and discover what the customer is feeling emotionally. What makes the customer happy? What makes the customer angry or upset? Knowing these answers will set you on the path to profitability.

A strong argument can be made that there's no substitute for sharing the customers' experiences firsthand, but the fact is, some of the most successful advice professionals have never experienced their clients' situations themselves. They've practiced The Empathy Effect by taking great pains to garner knowledge about their customers' wants and needs. Whether through first-hand experience or by accruing knowledge, business people giving empathetic advice know what the customer is really looking for. They can suggest ways to mitigate—and often eliminate—the customer's problems and make their experiences more positive. It's The Empathy Effect in action: The advisor feels empathy for the customer, which allows him to give relevant and constructive advice. The customer goes home and applies those suggestions, and soon benefits from the results. When the customer realizes that the advice was right on the money, he will hold the advice professional in great esteem. The customer places high value in the feeling of being taken care of, in the security of having an ally in his corner to help with a particular area of his life or business. The empathetic professional earns a devoted customer who will come back repeatedly to do business with his trusted advisor. It's a true win-win situation, and a perfect example of The Empathy Effect.

## Communicating the "Why"

Practicing The Empathy Effect in the advice business means answering your customers' questions before they're even asked. Whether the question is about your product or service or the problem it's supposed to solve, the customer wants to know *why* one choice or course of action is better than another, why it's important and necessary. The customer's need to understand the "why" only grows when your advice is not what they expected to hear—which often happens with the best advice professionals, who break the molds and suggest improvements over the status quo. For anyone in the advice business, communicating the "why" is huge.

## Three Layers of Empathy

In one form or another, being in the advice business means being in sales. You're not only selling your advice to customers, but you're selling them on the validity of your opinions and reputation—so that they'll hire you. Even highly qualified professionals like doctors, lawyers and accountants have to sell their services. We see their ads on television all the time. But many people who should be in the advice business—whether they actually are or not—are those that represent the first "B" in the sales progression from business-to-business (B-to-B), and then business-to-consumer (B-to-C). When you're in the position of that first B, you need to have empathy for both your initial customer and for your customer's customer. The first-B who offers the middle-B valuable advice on how to improve sales will naturally gain a larger share of the market.

To think past the initial customer to the consumer, salespeople need the multi-layered empathy to engage in a little "backwards thinking." The insight that leads to sales really starts at the business-to-consumer level, and then moves in reverse to the business-to-business level. That's when the communication really opens up. In a B-to-B situation, the conversation is always weaker when you focus solely on the B-to-B side. You'll have a far more meaningful exchange of ideas with your middle-B customer when you also know the B-to-C side of the business. It requires total empathy.

Take ketchup, as a hypothetical example. The product has three layers—manufacturer, distributor (grocery store or wholesaler), and consumer. The manufacturer represents the first B in the chain. If he's trying to sell his ketchup to the grocery store without knowing what the consumer really wants and needs, that lack of empathy will eventually bring him down. Mediocre players representing the first B don't think to offer sales advice to the middle B, because they're not thinking empathetically. Focused exclusively on the business-to-business transaction, they lose sight of the crucial business-to-consumer conclusion. Without empathy, the mediocre salesman spends his time trying to schmooze the middle-B, instead of offering the client suggestions for how to sell more effectively to the consumer.

"Look," the salesman says, "we've come out with a new-and-improved version—ketchup and mustard mixed together, in the same bottle!"

The product fails to sell, because the manufacturer doesn't understand what the consumer wants.

Heinz and Del Monte have shown empathy for the customer's experience by introducing ketchup bottles that can stand upside-down. They knew that consumers were frustrated by old fashioned ketchup bottles. It was almost impossible to get the last of the ketchup from the old bottles, and a pain in the butt to try and scrape it out with a knife. Consumers usually wound up throwing away some of the ketchup they had bought. The advent of squeezable plastic bottles that can stand inverted on the cap eliminated a nuisance for the consumer, making their experience of using ketchup more positive and warming the customer to the brand.

Now the manufacturer's rep can walk into the grocery store and say, "We understand the consumer's concerns. That's why we're introducing this new design, which we think will increase your sales by 30%." The first B has taken the time to understand the ultimate customer, and can help the middle-B sell more effectively.

The mediocre player never goes much deeper than saying, "Hey, how's it going?" He tries to take the client out for lunch or a round of golf, but never exercises the empathy that would make the client's job easier or his business more profitable. Without empathy and advice, the B-to-B relationship is shallow and cursory and won't stand the test of time. Why should it?

In my business, practicing The Empathy Effect would mean extending my understanding beyond the real estate agent and to the homebuyer. As a mortgage person who had formerly sold real estate,

I was in a good position to help both my Realtor lead sources and my home-loan customers. I knew from firsthand experience the issues that real estate agents face, especially during tough economic times. I understood their pain. I had walked in their shoes, and sometimes stumbled. If I could make it easier for the Realtor to please his clients and sell more homes, my company would be rewarded with an increase in sales. In the home-loan business, firsthand experience is almost a necessity for the salesperson. A renter who has never bought a home herself would have a difficult time advising a homebuyer about which mortgage option to choose. It's still possible to understand the homebuyer's point of view through diligent study, but this is one field where most people eventually have the experience themselves. Either way, if I'm going to sell a real estate agent on doing business with me, I've got to demonstrate a clear understanding of what the homebuyer is thinking about, and then relate that understanding back to the agent, and then back to myself. That's the circular nature of The Empathy Effect—and the key to success for people in the advice business. When you empathize with the middle-B and his customer, your client will appreciate your advice and reward it with continuing business—over years or even decades. It all starts with empathy.

By demonstrating empathy and insight, I would have a better relationship with my lead sources, setting myself apart from competitors who tried to mask their lack of knowledge with irrelevant attempts to impress the client: "Let me bring some donuts in here. Let me sponsor your next walk-a-thon." Superficial gestures might help close one transaction, but they don't build relationships.

## Remembering the End User

The key to giving meaningful business-to-business advice lies in understanding the end user. This depth of comprehension adds a layer past the buyer, possibly even beyond the consumer, all the way to the final user of the product or service. (The consumer is not necessarily the end user. If a mom is buying toys or snacks for her children, the kids will have the ultimate say in whether she purchases that brand again. They're the ones who have to like the product—and the people for whom the salesperson needs to have the most empathy.)

Consider public relations, an industry that occupies the first B in the sequence of B-to-B, and then B-to-C. To effectively advise the middle-B client, PR executives also have to have empathy for the end users. (In PR there are actually two layers of end users: the media targeted by publicity campaigns, and the consumer readers or viewers.) The best PR professionals not only possess a clear understanding of their clients' goals and challenges, and the messages the clients need to share with the public, but they also have empathy for the media people whom they target on behalf of their clients, and for the customers who are the audiences of those newspapers, magazines, radio and television stations, websites, etc. Consumers are the end users the clients want to reach through public relations. So what's the point of drumming up publicity if the client isn't saying something of value to the consumer? The advice that a PR firm gives to a client can't end at how to get quoted in the press—the real power of The Empathy Effect in public relations comes from understanding the needs and frustrations of the consumer who will read or view that publicity. That's the key to giving them something they can use. And it all starts with empathy.

Remembering the end user is huge for producers of entertainment products. Mark Burnett, the reality-TV whiz responsible for hit shows like "Survivor" and "The Apprentice," owes much of his success to understanding the end user—the viewer at home. Beyond selling the networks that buy his programs, Burnett has to know what his audiences will respond to in a new show. He has shown that he understands the nature of the consumer. He knew that people were tired of all the garbage sitcoms during primetime for our kids to see. Of course the reality-TV craze has unleashed some stupid, vile programs of its own—young women in bikinis lying in boxes while live rats are poured over their bodies, or prostituting themselves to millionaire strangers—but Burnett's winning formula has been to create competitive serials with real-life characters audiences can relate to. Viewers get hooked because they want to see what will happen next—

which contestants will be fired or voted off the island this week? The personalities chosen for the competitions mirror those that people find at school or work, from the affable hard workers to the scheming backstabbers that audiences love to hate. Being the first into the reality arena, Burnett wrote his own ticket and spawned a swarm of imitations that have mostly failed to resonate with viewers. Few have showed Burnett's mix of showmanship and empathy. As a producer pitching his product to the television networks, he had to convince the middle-B that he understood the tastes and preferences of the end users, the TV viewers. And he has hit some big home runs.

Needless to say, it takes a lot of effort to understand your customer, your customer's customer, and the end user. Most salespeople representing the first B, especially in small companies, won't make the commitment needed to gain all of that knowledge. Maybe they're afraid that professional research about customer preferences is too expensive, and lies beyond their means to acquire it. Even when you can't afford professional research, the Internet provides easier access to authoritative information than at any previous time in history. Nonetheless, it's the rare advice person who spends the time and money to learn about every layer, all the way down to the end user. But the ones that take the trouble become superstars.

## Educating the Client

When your customer is the middle-B in that B-to-B, B-to-C chain, one way to keep the empathy wheel turning is to always be providing the client with information that makes his job easier. It might seem counterintuitive, but the middle-B doesn't necessarily understand the consumer or end user, despite being one step closer to him. If you can present advice backed by solid statistics or research, especially when it reveals the emotional state of the end user, and you educate the middle-B on how to capture larger market share, then you become indispensable to the middle-B. Even on the first sales call, when you arm yourself with an understanding of the middle-B's customer, and more specifically if you demonstrate insight into the likes and needs of the end user, The Empathy Effect is set in motion for everyone involved.

"What I have here are the latest statistics on how these consumers are buying.... Black clothes are back for men.... Pink is the new color for women this year...."

When empathy enters the picture, you're not just in sales—you're in the advice business. "We've conducted a poll of people walking through the mall, and here's what we've found...."

One of the first steps in practicing The Empathy Effect for customers is to show that you're interested in their situation by asking a few questions: "Tell me about the challenges that you're facing. What's the one area of selling to your customers that gives you the most trouble?" If you can find solutions to their problems, then you are ready to educate the customer. Because the fact is, the customer needs to be educated—or at least to have his assumptions challenged, whether they're based on myths or not. So often salespeople are afraid to ask customers about the issues they're facing, thinking, "Oh well, the customer knows best. The customer is always right." But those clichés are simply not true. The customer knows what his challenges are, but he might not know how to solve them. That's why good, empathetic advice is so valuable.

Looking again at the example of public relations, a common problem is that the clients don't understand the service they're paying for. They haven't been educated about why they might need publicity or crisis management with the media, and how it can help their businesses. Early in their engagement with PR firms, many companies that have not been given empathetic advice don't understand the difference between public relations and advertising. They think the two services are one and the same. They want the press release announcing their company's latest news to read like an advertisement—popping off the page with lots of adjectives and exclamation points. The mediocre players will give the client what they want, instead of advising them on what they need. And lo and behold, they get no results. The media outlets ignore the client's story.

Meanwhile over at the empathetic PR shop, the superstar advice professional isn't afraid to tell the client why the course of action

they expect might not be in their best interests. Providing constructive, empathetic advice can mean telling the client things that, at least
at first, they might not want to hear. But the most empathetic pros
have the foresight to offer information upfront, to avoid having the
client become irritated and ask, "What do you mean, we can't say it
that way? We're paying for this press release, so we should be able to
word it however we want to!"

The empathetic PR practitioner explains beforehand why an
overtly promotional tone would backfire with the media. He clarifies
the difference between public relations and advertising for the client
right at the beginning, before a misunderstanding even has a chance
to develop.

"Since public relations is about communicating with consumers
through the news media, rather than directly through advertisements,
we've found that media people are more receptive to our messages,
and more likely to do stories on our clients, when we show empathy
by giving them information in their own language—in a style that
emulates a newspaper or magazine article. If we write your media cor-
respondence like ad copy, your message is more likely to wind up in
the waste basket than in the newspaper."

In media relations, another unpopular truth is that the client's
spokesperson must be available on short notice for interviews—and
with small, entrepreneurial companies, the spokesperson is often the
owner or CEO. The advice person working for the PR firm could
be timid and say, "I can't tell the company president that he has to
drop everything and be accessible on a moment's notice!" But that
timorous reluctance would not be empathetic for the ultimate goal.
The PR person has to have the conviction to give the client some
empathy about his own position: "I've got good relationships with
these reporters. When a news story is breaking and they're on dead-
line, they need expert sources to quote, and in a hurry. That's how we
can get your company into the paper in a positive light, and create a
good long-term relationship with the reporter."

In business, practicing The Empathy Effect means continually
educating the client, giving him the "why" over and over again, in an

empathetic way that doesn't insult his intelligence. And that requires an empathetic company culture, one that includes mechanisms for educating the customer. In the advice business, whether it's public relations or financial services, cooking supplies or home loans, clients are often unsure of what they want or need. It's the job of the business dispensing the advice to sort it out for them.

"I'm in a quandary here," the customer says (or maybe is just thinking to himself), "and I really don't know which choice is best for me."

"Well, that's okay," the empathetic advisor replies. "That's why you came to me. Now let me take you through this...."

## Tactful Advice

I spent a lot of time thinking about how The Empathy Effect goes through the first layer and touches the second—and possibly third—layers of a transaction. For the mutually beneficial phenomenon of The Empathy Effect to occur, the situation has to be empathetic on every level, not just on a select few. If I was going to give advice to the middle-B, even if it was rooted in empathy, I still had to be empathetic about how I communicated my advice. If I didn't choose my words carefully, I might offend someone by presuming to tell them how to run their business. I had to be tactful in my communication and respect my customer's understanding of his business and his own customer. I couldn't make assumptions about what my customers knew and did not know. Some middle-B clients might understand their end users better than others. I didn't want to come off sounding like I knew my lead source's business better than he did himself. That's just tact, which comes from empathy. Without empathy, there is no tact.

Practicing The Empathy Effect in the advice business means taking the trouble to understand your clients and how to communicate with them. Their personalities are all different. Some are impatient and want you to get straight to the point; others might find that approach abrupt and rude. Empathetic advice, I realized, is custom advice. Communicating with the customer is analogous to being a writer and knowing your audience. The *Chicago Sun-Times* writes its articles in a different tone than the *New York Times* does—based on the editors' knowledge of their respective readerships. In the advice business, communicating empathetically means respecting the customer's intelligence, circumstances and needs.

When your client is the CEO of a small company, he or she might have a big ego and feel too proud to want to listen to your advice. That's where The Empathy Effect takes even more hard work and understanding. When the client thinks he's King of the Hill, it becomes more challenging for the advice person to communicate tactfully. It requires more empathy. You also need that extra shot of empathy when the small-business CEO falls on hard times with his cash flow—telling yourself, "I have to roll with the punches here." Of course, it's also crucial that you choose the appropriate route for your business. If you realize that your culture is a mismatch for working with the heads of small companies, you might be better off pitching your services to a major corporation, where your contact is lower down the totem pole.

Regardless of the client's size, the empathetic advice professional tailors his message and terms appropriately. Nothing screams "LACK OF EMPATHY!" louder than a sales pitch that doesn't match its market. I remember a software salesman who tried to sell me a new system for $225,000. "Just want to let you know, this is going to be your cost," he said. Maybe the salesman was used to dealing with big companies, but his pitch was hopelessly off-target for a small, entrepreneurial businessperson like me. Obviously I wasn't going to write him a check for $225,000. Instead, I wound up buying my first two software licenses from a company that specialized in computer platforms for the mortgage business. Because he knew the industry, this salesman had total empathy for the small player. He had aligned himself with a lender to provide financing for his customers, because he could equate the cost of the software to a monthly payment, to make it more affordable. He was smart and empathetic, and he made sales as a result.

Sometimes people in the advice business don't really understand what their customer wants or needs, and maybe they don't even care. But if they're going to survive, let alone become superstars in their fields, then they have to develop empathy. Depending on what widget they're selling they might be able to muddle through for a while without caring what's important to the customer, but without empathy they'll never hit the big time.

A mortgage loan officer walks in to see a homebuilder, hoping the builder will agree to refer him business. To his credit, the mortgage guy has done his homework on the end user, but the problem is that he communicates it all wrong.

"Yeah, we know the consumer," he snorts, trying to seem like a real pro. "We know what they're buying and what they're not buying."

The builder resents the salesman's presumption, thinking, "Hey man, you're not in our business. Who are you to come in here and tell me about my customers?"

A more empathetic presentation—and I've often thought that presentation skills should be taught side-by-side with empathy—might center on new data and research from respected sources, or promise new research of its own.

"Let me sit down here in your sales center this weekend," the empathetic mortgage guy tells the homebuilder. "Let me call some of your past customers, so I can do my due diligence."

Even if the first-B has already done the research and gained an understanding of the middle-B's market, his pitch will be much stronger if he casts himself as a partner to help the client sell more of whatever it is that the client sells—whether it's homes, bottles of ketchup, or those boomerang paper airplanes that you see flying around in the mall.

Instead of marching into the middle-B's office and declaring, "Here's what your customer wants," a more tactful approach might be, "I've done my research, and I understand what your challenges are with your customers, based on your customer's needs and preferences. And I believe that I can help you overcome those challenges, so that you can increase your sales volume. Based on the results of this new research, I think I can make it easier for you."

Maybe he's got the results of a dozen surveys and focus groups showing what the consumer is looking for, but to be tactful the first-B still might ask, "Tell me about the issues you're facing with your customers." Often the middle-B client will welcome the chance to vent some steam. And if the first-B is practicing The Empathy Effect, he'll listen closely and be sure to respond to the client's specific concerns and frustrations. Even if both parties know the answer, The Empathy Effect flies out the window if the first-B insults the middle-B's intelligence. "Just want to let you know, I'm smarter than you are." Then he becomes unlikable—and that's no way for a salesperson to be.

## The Importance of Purpose

As I ruminated on The Empathy Effect, I realized that a strong sense of purpose is essential for anyone who gives customers advice for a living. You have to believe in what you're doing. And that requires confidence. Without empathy, the advice person will lack confidence, because he knows that he really doesn't understand his client's needs or situation. Maybe he tries to mask that lack of knowledge by acting cocky and strutting around. But when the person lacking empathy and confidence is challenged on what he's doing, he feels no courage for his convictions. He lacks a sense of purpose. Not honestly believing that his own advice is sound, he'll tend to back off. And then his credibility as an expert slurps down the drain.

The confidence that backs up a strong sense of purpose comes from knowing that you've either shared your clients' experiences, or you've put forth the effort to study and learn about their situations and needs.

My son-in-law, Tim Farritor, was running an office in Palm Beach Gardens, Florida, for my consulting company. It was his job to sell seats to my business seminars. His target market was owners of small mortgage companies who needed help to become more profitable. At first, Tim was having a tough time. Like any salesperson whose commissions depend on closing sales, he understandably felt pressure to perform. But he was keeping his gaze focused on the dollars, rather than on the needs of his customers. He made the mistake of pressing for commissions when he didn't have any empathy for his customers' situations.

In one of those ironic twists where I sometimes find myself consulting my own companies, I had to virtually force-feed him empathy for the customer.

"Let me explain to you what these people are going through, and how you might be able to help them save their businesses."

I had him interview some of the mortgage-company owners who were on the brink of having to shut their doors, so he could understand the problems they were facing. And sure enough, his sales shot up when he took his mind off the almighty dollar and started empathizing with the struggles that his clients were experiencing. Tim sold more seats when he thought about the pain that these people were going through and how the seminar could help them turn the corner, rather than staying focused on the commissions he might receive. Only then could he offer the empathetic advice that would generate sales.

After the seminar people were telling him, "Man, if I hadn't done this, I would have been out of business. No doubt about it."

When Tim had the chance to hear stories of his customers' experiences, he began to understand them even more empathetically. And as The Empathy Effect would have it, everybody benefited: The salesman became more confident and gained a greater sense of purpose, thereby increasing his sales. And the customers learned ways to boost—or even save—their businesses.

For anyone whose living depends in part on giving advice, the tools of customer interviews and surveys help create a more empathetic result. Getting inside the customer's head is especially important when you're first starting out in business. Without a clear understanding of the market you're trying to sell, you're lost in the woods without a compass. The goal is to get the customer to open up and share his or her experiences with you. "This is what happened to me." What I found is that surveys don't necessarily provide blanket solutions, but instead help identify niches of customer need. Because again, empathetic advice is custom advice. Whether giving recommendations to business owners or consumers, we had to constantly increase our competency by having the open-mindedness to understand and empathize with the customers' particular situations. "We've got to open this thing up as wide as possible," I told myself. "When I'm trying to accumulate this knowledge so I can feel empathy for the client, I can't be limited by tunnel vision or myopia." I had to take the blinders off and open my peripheral vision, to look around and really absorb what I was seeing. Only then could I truly understand the customers, and create empathy-based USPs they would appreciate.

## Price Business, or Advice Business?

I remember a story about a business owner whose firm was retained to plan a high-profile media event for a major new client. He had won the contract by bidding lower than the competition—which in retrospect would stand out as the first sign of trouble. This guy had been in business a long time and knew a thing or two about event-planning and publicity, but he had a reputation for arrogance and a lack of tact and respect for others.

Nonetheless, the client, who was known for being rich but penny pinching, went for the low-ball bid. Maybe the vendor figured the client was more interested in price than in advice—if he had even taken the trouble to think about it that much. Thanks largely to the talents of his staff, he managed to deliver an excellent event and media coverage for the new client. But with no underlying sense of empathy, the relationship soon crumbled.

When the bill arrived, the fledgling client was shocked to find that it was five times higher than the estimate he'd agreed to in the contract. "I couldn't believe my eyes," he said. "Was this guy kidding me?"

It turns out that at some point during the planning of the event, one of the vendor's employees had asked the client which of two choices he preferred for some catering detail. One of the options was more expensive than the other, but the client had answered, "Do whatever it takes to make this thing work."

Seizing upon that glib response, the client decided he had carte blanche to begin piling on billings far above the scope of the initial agreement. Too many of his employees logged too many hours work-ing on the event, and in the end the business owner thought he could charge the new client for every last penny of that time.

"You'd better pay this bill," he demanded arrogantly when the cli-ent called to contest it. "You said we should do whatever it took to deliver a great event, and this event was a smash success. So pay up."

He had no tact, no empathy, and wasn't willing to take any responsibility for the runaway train of his staff's hourly billings. Rather than keeping the client's point of view in mind, and having the empathetic diplomacy to work out a solution to the bill that had swollen out of control, he was only worried about what he could get for himself. Maybe he saw it as an opportunity to make a bundle off a big-name client. Or maybe his arrogance was just a front for the guilt he was feeling for doing something that he knew wasn't right. But lo and behold, his association with the new client was permanently severed. "I'll never work with that guy again," the client would say later. It was a classic example of ego ruining what might have otherwise been a long and mutually fruitful relationship. The crazy thing was that the vendor had only low-balled the bid in the first place because he was hoping that after the event was over he could get the client's long-term business. "They did great work," the client said, "but when the bill came, the situation turned real ugly, real fast." Just as a little empathy goes a long way, a clear lack of it can cause lots of damage.

The relationship might have been salvaged if the vendor had given the client some warning that the bill was growing out of control. "It would have made all the difference in the world if he had called mid-way through the project and said, 'Listen, I just want to let you know what's happening here, so we can work something out,' or if he had been willing to absorb some of the extra charges for the sake of our re-lationship going forward. Maybe we'd still be working together today."

With his blatant lack of empathy, the business owner not only killed his relationship with the high-profile client, but he also hurt his own reputation. The client he alienated might tell 20 other people in their field what happened, and soon word will spread through their surprisingly small community of businesspeople. Maybe the former client takes an executive position at another big company that could have become a new account for the vendor, or he plays golf with a fellow bigwig and tells him the story. The cumulative effect of reputation multiplies exponentially for the good or for the bad, often on the basis of empathy.

## Tilting the Pinball Machine

As I fought to liberate my mortgage company from the industry's price-based norm of bad customer service, I found that educating the consumer would mean finding the courage to tilt the pinball machine. The best players risk bumping the sides of the machine, to get more action from the ball. They know they might tilt and lose a few points. But the willingness to take that chance is what makes them great players. The mediocre player, on the other hand, is satisfied with a mediocre score, and doesn't take the chance that might improve it.

To really empathize with the consumer and make things easier for her, I might have to give advice that would run contrary to everything she had been taught by the industry norm. Because my advice was unusual, people might doubt its validity—but I couldn't buckle for fear of scaring the customer away.

As a real estate agent, I ran into a common customer misconception. When people are selling one home and buying another, they might have 80% equity in the first house. They've been taught that they have to roll all of their equity into the down payment on the new home, to avoid paying heavy taxes on the capital gains. But what many consumers didn't know was that in 1997, taxpayer relief allowed that a married couple could sell a home every two years without paying tax on the capital gains, as long as they weren't more than half-a-million dollars. The general public was largely unaware of the new rule. The belief in the marketplace remained the same as before, and people thought they had to roll all of their equity from home to home. It was simply wrong information. The consumer needed an advice person with enough empathy to educate them about the benefits of this obscure new law. But the mediocre players in the mortgage business weren't willing to upset the apple cart. They didn't want to challenge the consumer's misconception. "Oh well, the customer is always right. I'll just go along with them putting $300,000 into this $500,000 house."

What if the customer getting ready to roll over all of that equity also happened to be saddled with $25,000 in high-interest credit card debt? Maybe they had suddenly been hit with $100,000 in medical bills, or had to pay for an elderly parent's care in a pricey nursing home. They might need to tap some of that equity in their home to alleviate pressure in other areas of their financial life—and to receive the maximum financial return and benefit from the accumulated asset represented by that equity. If we're truly going to be experts in our business, to be advisors at the top of our game, then we've got to constantly accrue knowledge about matters that affect our customers, and to have the tact and empathy to communicate our recommendations for their best courses of action.

## Give It to Me Straight, Doc

If there's one field that's rife with client misconceptions, it's medicine. Unfortunately, healthcare has also become a sector with one of the lowest levels of empathetic communication and advice. The good advice that should help dispel patient misconceptions just isn't there, even in the part of people's lives where they need it the most. How many people still ask doctors for antibiotics to treat the common cold? They're looking for the quick fix, and not thinking about what lies beyond that. The doctor knows that colds and flu are viruses, and that antibiotics don't work against viruses, only against bacterial infections. Antibiotics are not only ineffective against the common cold, but might actually harm the patient's health. The doctor knows that antibiotics should be used sparingly, and only when absolutely necessary. Beyond the wasted money and nasty side effects, there are the bigger-picture implications posed by an uninformed public demanding antibiotics to treat their colds. When the medicines are mis-prescribed, germs can become resistant so that the antibiotics won't work in the future when the patient really needs them. It's not just the individual patient who suffers from misuse of these medicines, but society as a whole—every time the genie of antibiotics is let out of the bottle and set loose against the world's populations of bacteria, the more those germs have the chance to grow accustomed to the antibiotics, and come back even stronger than before. The drug companies find themselves in a constant scramble to come up with new antibiotics to replace the old ones that no longer work.

Many doctors go ahead and prescribe the antibiotics anyway, because they're scared of losing the patient. The doctor is afraid to tilt the pinball machine. He's worried that if he doesn't acquiesce to his patient's demands, the patient won't come back and will give his business to another doctor instead. The irony is that once the patient eventually finds the right advice person, he'll drop the doctor who wrongly prescribes the antibiotics anyway. The doctor who's afraid to tilt the pinball machine—or anyone meekly clinging to a flawed status quo, in any field—is going to be mediocre. In any advice business, if you want to score heavily, to the highest degree, you need the courage to give meaningful, empathetic advice, even if you risk rocking the boat. The doctor who really has a higher purpose, the one who will be a leader, has the intestinal fortitude to say, "Stop the insanity." And that's the doctor who will gain the most patients over time, through the phenomenon of The Empathy Effect.

Bedside manner is not taught in medical schools, because tact for doctors is not considered important. And that's thanks to a lack of empathy—and the fear of malpractice lawsuits that prods doctors to bluntly inform their patients of every terrifying, worst-case scenario for their health. Medical schools don't teach The Empathy Effect, but the best doctors are naturally empathetic with their patients. They know that they have to educate patients about the realities of antibiotics and the common cold—whether through one-on-one consultations, pamphlets and written materials, Internet seminars, e-mail newsletters or a FAQ on the physician's website, "Common Myths about Antibiotics and the Common Cold." Maybe the doctor writes a health column for a local newspaper, as a forum for his empathetic advice. Editors are usually receptive to guest columns framed as advice to readers. If a doctor truly empathizes with his patients, he'll realize that he has a great opportunity to help them by explaining when they need antibiotics and when taking the medicine would be bad for their health. Not only does the empathetic physician tell his patients that he doesn't prescribe antibiotics for head colds—more important, he explains why not. The doctor needs to be front-and-center with that information, and empathize with what the patient is thinking. Rather than just throwing his hands up in resignation and saying, "Oh, well, I'll have to write a prescription for this patient's cold. That's just the way it is," the best doctors have the empathy to help their patients help themselves. They have the opportunity to help change the way their patients think, for the better.

Too often, the doctor or other advice professional doesn't explain things right. They don't take the time. And most people are afraid to ask too many questions, thinking they'll embarrass themselves in front of the highly educated professional. But the empathetic physician will answer the "why" before it's even asked. "You're probably going to ask me, 'How come you don't just prescribe antibiotics for this cold?' Well, that's a great question, and as a matter of fact, I'm going to tell you the reason. I'm going to explain why it would be bad for your health if I did write that prescription. And on your way out, my assistant will also give you some literature on the subject, and the address of our website, where you can learn more about it."

Superstars in the advice business must seem like mind-readers to their clients, addressing the "why" before the customer even has a chance to wonder about it. That's empathy, putting yourself in the other person's shoes.

In my field, mortgage people seldom educate their customers and explain the "why." Like some doctors, they don't want to tilt the pinball machine. They follow the easy assumption, that every customer should take a 15-year, fixed-rate loan. But what if the customer would be better off with an interest-only loan? While they're making the interest payments every month, they're also taking what would have been the principal portion of their monthly payment and investing it into an interest-earning account that compounds over time. When the term of the loan is finished, they've paid off all the interest on the mortgage, and there's more than enough in the side account to pay off the principal, with money left over. It's a whole different perspective.

## Keeping Current, Looking Ahead

The empathy required to stay tactful when sharing information with customers coincides with the fact that, as an expert, you are constantly reading and acquiring new knowledge in your field. The customer might not be up-to-date on the latest developments, rules and regulations, economic news, or new innovations that affect the product or service that you offer. The best people in the advice business practice The Empathy Effect by making their customers' lives easier, and that means taking the time to stay current. But, notoriously, people who are supposed to be in the advice business don't keep abreast of the latest news and developments affecting their customers, the ones they're supposed to be advising. The mediocre players don't read and accrue knowledge. They're stuck in the past of their businesses. "I've been in this industry for 23 years, and this is the way we've always done things." They think they're the pros, and know everything there is to know about their fields. But no business is that simple. The playing field is constantly being redrawn—public tastes shift, markets change directions, new technologies and new rules govern the game. When an advice person falls into a smug attitude with their decades of experience, they're apt to be crushed by the young Turks who eventually will come thundering through the system, armed with a superior understanding of consumer sentiments and trends. If you're not fresh with your knowledge and constantly modifying your advice to suit changing realities, you begin losing your ability to offer empathetic services, even with the best of intentions.

Resistance to market changes is an anti-empathy effect. It's a stubbornness that ignores or fights against the will of the consumer. More than ever as technology speeds forward in a blur, consumers' buying habits are also in constant flux—during the last 25 years the most popular music format has gone from vinyl records to CDs to MP3s. Where music fans once relished elaborate packaging on the albums of their favorite artists, now portability and the freedom to easily store and retrieve huge numbers of digital songs is more important to the music-buying public. Even if you don't prefer the latest trends for yourself as a consumer, as a businessperson creating The Empathy Effect you have to be broad-minded and magnanimous enough to accept whatever your market has come to prefer. Resistance to change is mostly driven by pride and fear—negative emotions that will undermine The Empathy Effect every time. Learning to set aside fear, pride and anger can make the difference between a fulfilled and prosperous life and one that's a bitter failure.

Part of practicing The Empathy Effect with customers means being open-minded about new consumer trends. Imagine when bottled water first hit the market. "You've got to be kidding me. No one's going to pay a dollar for a little bottle of water. They can get it from the tap for free!"

## Instilling Empathy

I wondered—are some people just naturally more empathetic than others? Are their personalities instinctively predisposed to empathy? Is there an empathy gene—and one for selfishness, too? Maybe some people are more empathetic because of their upbringings and life experiences. Those who have experienced pain can appreciate it in others. Or maybe they just become bitter.

If a person lacks empathy for some reason, then he or she is probably close to not being in sales at all. But I think anyone can learn to understand empathy, and to practice The Empathy Effect. If some people will never excel at sales, it's probably because they have some other talent in life. But I think that learning empathy can definitely improve a salesperson's chances for success. Somebody might be a six on a scale of one-to-ten, but if they're taught The Empathy Effect for the customer and end user, they can still become a sales superstar. So often the sixes end up staying at that level, because they're not taught what's really important, which is empathy. In sales, people can learn to adopt a style, even an empathetic one, if only because their survival depends on it. Of course an empathy charade won't work, but after being shown the principles of empathy the salesperson might begin to feel them for real. Again it comes down to the "why," except this time it's the salesperson, and not the customer, who needs that explanation. What's the reasoning behind it? Any up-and-coming salesperson can learn to do business more empathetically when he's shown why it's so important. Too often a person's potential for sales is dismissed—"Well, they just don't fit the profile,"—after being judged against an accepted standard like the DISC test, the behavioral and personality evaluator developed by psychologist William Moulton Marston in 1928. The "D" stands for Dominance, "I" for Influence, "S" for "Steadiness," and "C" for Conscientiousness. A person ranked a high-I for influence is considered to have the best disposition for sales. But if you were to teach a high-S or a high-C the "why," they could adapt their style to become a learned "I," strong on influencing others. The person could become a better salesman, if not a natural born one, rather than thinking that he just doesn't have what it takes to sell. Teaching empathy instills confidence. Environment also plays a big role. Someone might be encouraged to pursue a career in sales because of their parents' influence, or other people telling them, "You're a natural born salesman." This kind of positive reinforcement has a way of influencing the brain for the better—a true Empathy Effect. (The value of positive reinforcement is especially evident when contrasted with its opposite, the damaging practice of trying to discourage others.) Lo and behold, the person who's been encouraged turns out to be talkative and friendly. But if someone is really passionate and wants to learn sales, to adapt to sales, I think they can succeed by learning The Empathy Effect for the end user. Accruing that knowledge will make them more confident. The positive force of that confidence washes forward over everything it touches—the sale, the payday, the customers' satisfaction, your reputation and future business, and so on.

## The Role of Emotional Intelligence

Sometimes when you have empathy, people think you're smarter than you really are. They judge your intelligence level as high because you've figured out what they need and how to deliver it to them. What comes across as shrewdness might really be empathy. Maybe a person is not very smart at all—he just has lots of empathy for people, which they equate to intelligence. Of course, there are different definitions of "smart," like book smarts and street smarts. Empathy falls more into the category of emotional intelligence, which can be more valuable than formal learning. But when you combine education—through academic degrees or self-study—with emotional intelligence, it's a powerful swing that can knock the ball out of the park, right onto Waveland Avenue. Someone who comes straight from college with book smarts but no emotional intelligence is at a disadvantage, until they realize through empathy and experience how that book learning fits with understanding what the customer wants and needs.

## Letting Empathy In

A common trap for people in the advice business is that, because of their education and expertise, they begin to feel superior to the clients. And they lose their empathy. "The client just doesn't get it," they tell themselves. "The client is ignorant." The person who should be dispensing empathetic advice instead develops an arrogant contempt for his customers. The relationship becomes adversarial under the surface. The vendor is now intimidating to his clients, the very people for whom he should be feeling empathy. Intimidation and ego are the polar opposites of empathy, and direct threats to the long-term profitability of any business.

If it's true that empathy can be taught, then it's equally important that the student be willing to make the shift towards understanding and appreciating the situations of others. In the absence of some life-altering event, you have to want to change. For people who have always been driven by thoughts of themselves and their own desires, the first step is to let go of ego.

Let's say there are four quadrants in your brain—or your psyche, or soul. If all four quadrants are filled with ego, empathy can't get in there. If you haven't been raised to think empathetically, the alternate course is to push out ego and create an empty space, so that empathy can enter. Of course that's no easy task, and the older you get the harder it becomes. Learning empathy might have to begin as a conscious mental exercise rather than a natural emotional response—when a situation arises where your own needs and convenience are pitted against doing what's right for another person, you almost have to catch yourself and evoke the discipline to check your habitual impulses. After establishing a pattern of these conscious choices away from selfishness or ego, you might find that empathy begins to come more naturally. When someone is self-centered and egotistical, without empathy, they probably know in their heart of hearts that being that way is causing them harm. If he's honest with himself, an egotistical person can look back and see the damage that his lack of empathy has caused to his life and career over the years. And that realization might be just the push he needs to begin thinking more empathetically.

## Survival of the Most Empathetic?

In the absence of a monopoly, which businesses prosper and which ones fail can come down to Survival of the Most Empathetic. An entrepreneur might have empathy at the beginning, when he's struggling himself, but as time goes by and he becomes more successful, that sense of empathy might begin to erode. In some cases, the mere passage of time can chip away at the empathy that a person or a business feels for others. People become tired and fall into ruts of routine and stagnation. And then some calamity has to occur to yank them out, to humble them back into empathy.

It's the same for people who have always led ego-driven lives. Often they won't become more empathetic unless some catastrophe forces the change. Their business might suffer a serious setback, maybe even sink into bankruptcy—one way or another, they're whacked over the head with a 2 x 4: "Holy crap, we're not as good as we thought we were."

If the business owner finds his best clients deserting him, he might begin to see things in a different light. Maybe he'll feel compelled to reassess his assumptions and ingrained behaviors, to begin operating from a new, and perhaps more empathetic, point of view. Developed through stages of life, arrogance is a form of limited vision. Setbacks in business can make us remove the blinders, for our own good. A failure can be like a forest fire that improves the health of the ecosystem—ash fertilizes the soil, and from the black ruins, bright wildflowers grow.

Maybe someone's number-one client has decided to take her business elsewhere. But when a person is humbled, ego is removed, so empathy can enter.

"Wow, I guess I really do need to understand my customers better.... Maybe it's time for me to focus more on their needs, and less on my own...."

Ironically, it's not until you become more empathetic to others that you can really help yourself.

## Chapter Four

# *Empathy and the Three Levels of Customer Satisfaction*

The way I see it, once any business acquires a new customer, there are three possible levels of satisfaction for that person or client. Which of the three levels the customer finds herself at depends largely on the amount of empathy present within the company.

Level One is when a new customer first comes aboard. This is the honeymoon phase, the romance period. From the customer's perspective the relationship is fresh and exciting. It seems full of promise. The customer feels taken care of, and no flaws or problems have had a chance to pop up yet.

Let's say the business is a bank. At Level One, the customer's main contact might still be just her personal banker and that person's assistant. Within the limited sphere of that relationship, everything runs beautifully. There's a chemistry between the vendor and the customer. The accountholder feels a rapport with her personal banker, a sense of empathy that leads to trust. She hasn't had to deal with people in other departments of the bank yet. For the time being at least, she can imagine being a loyal customer for years to come.

Now it's six months later. The honeymoon euphoria has faded. The customer is still satisfied, if no longer giddy with excitement. This is Level Two, a crucial phase for the future relationship between the company and the customer. The experiences the customer has at Level Two will determine whether she ascends to Level Three, or becomes disappointed and decides to take her business elsewhere.

Level Two is critical because it's when the customer begins to see beyond the smiling face of her primary contact, to glimpse what goes on behind the scenes at the organization—like Dorothy pulling back the heavy drape to reveal the truth about The Wonderful Wizard of Oz. Maybe the customer has occasion to interact with employees in the bank's other departments, like the representatives who answer calls to its 800 number. Will these strangers provide the same warmth and great service that the familiar and friendly personal banker does? Or will they disappoint the customer with rude attitudes, indifferent service, broken promises and mistakes? Whether the bank's infra-structure can sustain the great experience the customer enjoys with her primary contact depends on whether the company as a whole has an empathetic culture.

## Come Fly with Me

Only those organizations that consistently provide the best experi-ences and quality will earn the right to elevate their customers to Level Three. At this higher altitude, the customer is completely blown away by a product or service that always exceeds her expectations. She becomes a raving fan of the business.

"This is the greatest banking relationship I've ever had," she says. "And I'm so pleased that I'm going to refer all of my friends and family to you, too. If anybody asks, I'll say that you guys are the best bank-ers in the world, that you really take care of your customers. I'll give people your number and tell them who to call."

At Level Three, the relationship with the customer takes on a whole new meaning. Rather than becoming disillusioned when she sees past her primary contact and begins dealing with other people and departments in the company, the customer instead grows even more impressed as she begins to discern the empathetic culture that pervades the entire organization. When a company's culture is based on empathy—between the employees and the customers, the manage-ment and the employees, the company and the community and among the employees for one another—the organization becomes unified and seamless. No matter where the customer might intersect with the company, she will always have a great experience. From the tellers upfront to the backroom staff supporting them, from the personal banker to the people answering phones at the 800 call center, there's a ribbon of empathetic continuity throughout the organization.

When your customer first emerges from the heady honeymoon phase of Level One, it's essential that your company performs at its best to elevate her straight to Level Three. You've got to keep knocking the ball out of the park—and without using a corked bat. A company that can deliver the genuinely superlative experiences that lift customers to Level Three will be rewarded with a continuous stream of referrals—and the organization will grow, and grow and grow. That's The Empathy Effect in action.

## Is There Empathy in the Backroom?

A company might succeed in keeping its customers aloft at Level Three for a long time. But whether that relationship stays strong or begins to weaken depends on the performance of the organization's backroom. (In some industries, "the backroom" might refer to the production department; at Majestic Mortgage, it's our operations department.) This is where the presence or absence of empathy really makes or breaks the company's customer service.

No matter how stellar a performer the customer's primary contact might be, and even if this person was solely responsible for acquiring the customer in the first place, he or she alone won't be able to sustain the customer at Level Three without strong and empathetic backroom support. Even if the customer slides back down to Level Two, where she's still satisfied but no longer wowed, it could be that the only thing preventing her from leaving is that one great employee who's holding it all together for her. A few glitches might occur here and there, but the customer still feels that the business is meeting her needs in general.

"I hit a few speed bumps with the bank," she says, "but they weren't enough to rip off the tires. I'll probably keep my accounts here because of my representative. He listens to me and understands my concerns. When something goes wrong, even in a different department, I know he'll take care of it for me."

For the customer, it makes a huge difference to have an ally in the company who will sort out any problems that might arise. But that great employee's best efforts can only go so far when there's no empathy in the backroom or in the overall company culture. If mistakes continue to sour the customer's experience, one of two things will eventually happen. The customer might become fed up and lose confidence even in her great representative, because that person can't perform in the non-empathetic environment of the company. "Maybe this place really isn't so great after all," the disaffected customer tells herself. "I think I'll start looking around to see what else is out there."

The other possibility is that the salesperson becomes as sick of the situation as the customer is. The representative says, "Enough is enough," and leaves. He might have suspected that his customers were going to start disappearing anyway, because of all the backroom screw-ups, so he tells himself, "Maybe I should just leave first, and try to take some of my customers with me. If they're all going to stop doing business here I won't be able to make a living anyway, so I might as well go first and blame the organization for all of the errors that happen here. I'll promise my customers a better experience at my next employer's company."

If the customer believes she can count on her representative to straighten out the backroom's mistakes, and then that person leaves, who's she going to call? "I thought I had problems before, but just look at this mess now!" She ends up following the employee to his next position, if only because she prefers the devil she knows to the one she doesn't know. "A change has to be made, so I might as well go with John. He's familiar with my situation. He knows my idiosyncrasies."

So now the poorly run, non-empathetic backroom is causing the company to lose both its customers and its best salespeople. There's no tenure with the sales staff, and this lack of continuity and employee experience further erodes customer satisfaction and longevity. Around and around it goes, in a downward spiral.

In any business, it's essential that employees in the backroom understand that they might be the ones controlling whether the company generates referrals. And because of the enormous effect they have on the customer's experience, the backroom staff also controls the company's growth. Management has to emphasize and pay close attention to what goes on in the backroom. Are the processes empathetic for the sales force and the customer? The Empathy Effect should be taught throughout the company's culture, from the backroom forward.

Management has to give people in the backroom the opportunity to fully understand the vital cause-and-effect nature of their work. It means having empathy for the backroom staff themselves: When shown the importance of their jobs, they start to take more pride in their work, which then raises standards within the organization and leads to better service and higher customer satisfaction. When the employees feel pride and really dig into their jobs, they shine in front of their peers and begin to move up the corporate ladder.

"Wow, look at Mary! She's really done well for herself."

Her purpose was to take care of the customer, and she also understood that something as seemingly small as a mistake on a change-of-address form could potentially alienate a client and send destructive ramifications all down the line—affecting the company's profitability and shareholder value, undermining the entire organization and everyone associated with it. Her awareness of the big picture comes back to the vision that's tied to empathy—the ability to recognize the effects that your attitudes and actions will have on other people.

The indicators of a badly run backroom might be that customers are leaving or the company is losing market share. Maybe the company hasn't kept up with the times or is no longer providing a great experience for its staff, so the employees become discouraged and start letting their work slide. And sometimes, of course, the problem isn't that the backroom is failing the frontline salespeople, but the other way around—the salesperson might promise the customer something that the backroom can't deliver.

"Oh, sure," the salesman tells the client. "We can have that order shipped out to you by Friday!"

When the backroom people hear that the salesperson has made a commitment they can't sanction, stress levels start to rise. "What do you mean, it has to go out on Friday? You know we don't have any trucks going out on Friday!"

"But I already promised the customer, so somebody has to do it!"

What follows is a scene from The Keystone Kops—the entire staff frantically rushing around to fulfill the salesperson's promise. Mistakes lead to discounting and a tarnished company image, undercutting profitability and threatening to send the customer sliding down to a lower level of satisfaction, if not straight out the door.

## As Levels Drop, Referrals Stop

Customers happily sailing along at Level Three will be almost evangelistic in their zeal for referring others to your company. So it makes sense that one of the first signs of trouble is when those referrals start drying up. It shows that customers are slipping off the perch of Level Three and have somehow become disappointed or dissatisfied with your company. People don't want to recommend a company that's going to give their friends, family or colleagues a bad experience. They have their own reputations to consider. How would such bad advice reflect on the person giving it?

"Thanks a lot, Bob. You recommended this bank to me, and now my wife wants to divorce me. They mailed the wrong statement to my house, and she hit the ceiling when she opened the envelope."

When people who used to refer your company stop doing so, chances are that a lapse in your organization's empathy is causing the problem. And it will take some proactive empathy to pull those foul balls back into fair play. Somebody within the organization has to notice that the customer who was formerly making referrals by the dozen has suddenly stopped giving them altogether. As usual, a little empathy goes a long way. "Is there something wrong?" The customer will probably appreciate the gesture. "Am I ever glad that you asked!" Maybe it's just that the customer's brother-in-law has entered the same business, and now the referrals are going to him instead. But it's important to at least investigate and find out what's going on.

In the absence of some major, catastrophic screw-up that instantly alienates customers, when a company starts losing clients they'll probably slide down in stages, just as they had earlier risen level by level. It's unlikely that the customer will abruptly go from being blown away at Level Three to suddenly saying, "That's it, I'm done." The client is more likely to gradually lose confidence in the company through an accumulation of errors. Once they start falling, you have to work tremendously hard and perform far beyond expectations to lift the customers back up to a higher level, and to overcome the negative perceptions created by the missteps that caused them to slide down in the first place. Once again, it all comes back to empathy. The problem will never be solved until you figure out what the customer is feeling, what they want and what they need. And then, of course, you have to deliver those things. But part of the vision involved with empathy means gathering that intelligence and acting on it at the beginning, not later in catch-up mode after a problem has developed. And it's precisely that kind of forward-looking understanding of other people's needs that helps keep customers at the apex of Level Three.

## Sustaining a "Level Three" Culture

If you establish a company culture with a clear mission statement that shows your organization really cares about its customers, then you should be able to elevate them to Level Three. And if an employee violates that culture—by being rude to a customer on the telephone, for example—then you might see a "citizen's arrest" from a more conscientious employee who witnesses the infraction against the company's empathy-based values.

"Hey listen, you really should not have told that customer to drive to the bank to solve their problem. You should have taken care of it for them. That was a huge breach of what this company stands for."

A culture of empathetic customer service sustains itself even when the manager is not around. Without those established standards, the other people on the staff might just roll their eyes at an employee's rude behavior toward customers. "Oh well, that's just Jane." And in a situation like that, the customer probably won't take the trouble to complain to the management—she'll just become dissatisfied and begin dropping to a lower level, on her way to becoming a former customer.

Excellent service starts with empathy—for the customer and internally within the company. If antipathy is corroding the relationship between the backroom staff and their managers, then the employees might become bitter and tell themselves, "You know what? Forget this place. I'm going to find some way to sabotage it. I don't care if the company loses customers, because I have no future here anyway. In fact, I've already started looking for a new job, and will give my notice as soon as I find one."

Internal empathy can't be selective; it has to pervade the entire organization. It won't work to say, "We're going to have empathy over here, but not over there." Empathy has to benefit everyone involved—otherwise, there is no Empathy Effect. It might take a while to soak through your organization, but once that standard of empathy has been established, you've created an infrastructure that's hard to break. New hires will be mentored by people already steeped in the company's empathetic culture.

As a company grows, and especially as it expands into new geographical areas, management has to work extra hard to maintain empathetic customer service. Activities that used to be performed at the local level—and perhaps with a more personal and friendly touch—might be consolidated in another state. Maybe you're creating an 800-number call center for customer inquiries and complaints, instead of handling those functions locally. Suddenly the customer's experience is going to change—they've been used to calling their local representative and getting right through, and now they're forced to navigate a maze of voice-mail options, none of which is a precise fit for what they need, and then to sit on hold before finally talking to a stranger. Whether the person answering that call is friendly and helpful or curt and indifferent becomes a major factor in determining the level of the customer's satisfaction. Again it's a situation where empathy for the employee helps create empathy for the customer. The people answering those calls have to be set up for success—and a strong sense of purpose.

"I want you to know that you play a very important role here. Let me show you what could happen if your job is not carried out the right way."

As always, the ability to create an empathetic company culture is helped by an employee profit-sharing plan. Otherwise, the backroom people might become cynical and respond, "If my job is so important, then why aren't you paying me more?!"

When given a financial stake in the company's success, employees will naturally be more motivated to provide great customer service— empathy driving empathy. In a publicly traded company, an empathetic culture also leads to increased shareholder value and return. Since the employees often own stock in the company themselves, they have another motivation to consistently deliver at Level Three. "Man, this really does affect me."

## The Perils of Non-Empathetic Growth

For an example of the disorganization and rapid decline in customer service that can occur as a company grows, look no further than Washington Mutual. As the mortgage and banking giant's locations multiplied like dandelions, its customers soon found themselves stuck in the weeds. Beginning in early 2001, the Seattle-based company went on a massive acquisition spree, absorbing two large banks and the mortgage arms of three others. Thousands of homeowners who had formerly sent their monthly mortgage payments to other servicing companies would now send them to Washington Mutual instead. The company's loan-servicing portfolio suddenly quadrupled, swelling to $744 billion, according to SmartMoney.com. But Washington Mutual seemed more interested in how it could benefit from its gigantic expansion than it was in serving its customers. The acquisitions of so many far-flung entities had created a chaotic tangle of mismatched computer systems and infrastructure. Serious errors and horrendous service began to plague the company's customers. Checks were lost or returned, and customers who had never missed a mortgage payment suddenly began receiving notices threatening foreclosure unless their payments were brought up to date. "It was a horrid, nightmarish experience," SmartMoney quoted a former Washington Mutual customer as saying. People found themselves sunk into a bureaucratic morass as they tried without success to correct the problems with the company. "You not only received all of my payments on time, but you cashed them. I have the cancelled checks right here. So how can you be charging me late fees and threatening to foreclose on my house?" Service reps on the phone would tell customers that their computers showed no problems with their payments, and that everything would be fine. And then, a week later, the customer would hear a knock on the door and be served with a notice of default, announcing the bank's plans to foreclose. People who had repeatedly faxed cancelled checks to Washington Mutual to verify their payments were given notice that their homes would be put up for auction. They were scared to death, especially the company's elderly customers.

Because of Washington Mutual's bogus delinquencies, its customers' credit ratings were ruined. As the new servicer on people's home loans, the company also became responsible for making property-tax payments from escrow accounts. But the payments were often missed or late, and the escrow accounts were bungled. When customers wrote letters to the company, they received no response. "It was shocking and insulting how they treated us," one customer said. Coinciding with its unchecked growth, the company had launched an edgy advertising campaign that tried to lure young consumers with the suggestion that Washington Mutual was a cool, hip place to park their money. After the problems started, the ads were revealed to be misleading at best, horse manure at worst—unless endless errors and nightmarish service had somehow become cool and hip.

Boiled down to its essence, the problem with Washington Mutual was about greed and ego, and a complete lack of empathy. The company hadn't built a sound backroom infrastructure before launching its aggressive expansion push. These lopsided priorities shouted ego: "Let's grow for our own benefit, and worry about the customers later." And lo and behold, that self-centered lack of empathy proved disastrous for the company—resulting in a torrent of customer complaints, lost business, lawsuits, bad publicity and a tarnished brand. To establish trust, any company needs to practice The Empathy Effect—which means putting the customers' needs ahead of its own.

## Wearing Down the Bar of Soap

At Level One, the customer's image of the company is like a new bar of soap: smooth and perfectly formed, with the "Ivory" logo carved pristinely into the top. But eventually, in the course of washing your hands, the clear definition of that logo begins to wear away. The same thing happens to a customer's image of a company after a series of mistakes and disappointments: The bar of soap erodes more and more, until one day it breaks into little fragments that they drop in the bathtub and can barely find. The customer might try to pick up the pieces, but they slip down the drain.

One instance in particular might not seem like a big deal. "So somebody forgot to release my mortgage. That's all right."

But when a different employee gives the same customer a hard time about a $14 credit she's owed for a box of misprinted personal checks, another layer of trust and good will erodes.

The customer dials the bank's 800 number. "Hello, I called last month because the bank printed my checks with the wrong zip code, and I was told that I would be given a credit for the $14 charge, along with a new box of checks. The person I spoke to said it was the bank's mistake and that they would make up for it."

"Yes, ma'am."

"But in the statement I received today, I see that I've been charged another $14 for the second box of checks, and I haven't been credited for the first $14."

Combined, the woman and her husband have a total of 17 differ-ent personal and commercial accounts with this particular bank. The woman is a long-standing and highly valuable customer, but the girl on the 800 line treats her like an anonymous stranger.

"Well, ma'am," she says, "I don't see it on my computer screen that you were charged twice. It's not in my records."

The customer feels demeaned, like the employee is doubting her honesty. "But I've got the last two statements right here," she says. "I'm looking at the charges right now."

"I'm sorry, ma'am," the girl sighs, "but there's nothing I can do about it. Here's my suggestion for you: I'll pull up a directory of all the bank locations in your area, and you can go to the branch that's closest to your home, so they can fix this problem for you."

Maybe the girl is new, or her days at the bank are numbered, but her apathetic attitude shows a complete lack of empathy—and more important, a failure within the company's culture. The customer has been with the bank far longer than the employee has, and she already knows where all of its branches are located. She could probably recite the different branches' hours of operation, and give driving directions to each one. The girl on the phone has no empathy for the customer's situation, let alone for the problem she's trying to solve. Far from being helpful, the employee is rude and lazy—she doesn't want to cor-rect the billing error herself, so she tells the customer to take care of it instead. How would the customer feel walking into her local bank and saying to the teller, "Um, a girl on your 800 line told me I should come here to fix this problem?" The people at the bank would prob-ably respond incredulously, "She told you *what?*" And then matters would just get worse, as antipathy develops between the departments and employees in the bank branch start resenting the people who an-swer the 800 lines. Of course the customer is not going to follow the girl's inane advice and drive to a branch to argue the double-charge for her checks. She ends up calling the 800 number again, except this time asks to speak with a supervisor. "I can see the double charge right here, ma'am," he tells her apologetically, obviously chagrined by the situation. "I'll go ahead and reverse it, and I'll also talk to the person you spoke with earlier." And all of this hassle is over a $14 item. Of course the real problem isn't the money, but the principle of the matter—and more fundamentally, an underlying lack of empathy within the company's culture.

## Too Many Duck Bites

The screw-up with the misprinted checks—and the bank's failure to credit the customer's account for the overcharge—is just one in a series of errors that have reflected a lack of empathetic continuity within the company's backroom operations.

The woman's husband is already feeling frustrated because the bank's website requires him to change his password after every ten log-ins. This customer is Internet-savvy and likes the convenience of checking his accounts online, but he's not too keen on having to constantly remember new passwords. Reflecting a lack of empathy for the customer, the website aggravates the person trying to log in, as they're confronted with a maddening error message: INVALID USER-NAME OR PASSWORD. The bank's unreasonable requirements have caused the error, but the customer is made to feel responsible for it. If the bank had exercised empathy, it would have foreseen this inevitable complication and the inconvenience that it causes for the customer. Because as always, empathy is about vision and anticipating how another person will feel in a given situation, or the effect that our actions will have on other people. Maybe the bank's intentions are good—they might be trying to protect the customer from Internet "phishing" and identity theft. But the requirement that customers constantly invent and remember new passwords places the burden for that protection on the customer, rather than on the company itself. So sure enough, the customer forgets the latest in a series of online passwords, and finds himself having to call the 800 number. He's forced to slog through a menu of irrelevant voice-mail prompts ("For a bunch of stuff you don't need, press One! For a list of other useless options, press Two!") and then sit on hold for five minutes listening to the bank's recorded advertisements for itself, before finally speaking to a representative. The customer is a busy man with a stressful life, and this nuisance is far from welcome.

"First I had to call because you didn't have the system set up correctly to email me my password," he says. "And now I have to call again because I've forgotten my new one."

The representative on the 800 line starts asking him questions: *What's your mother's maiden name? What's the name of your favorite pet?*

"I feel like the bank is trying to protect me from myself, like they're the government." Not only is the customer annoyed and embarrassed, but this call is also tying up his valuable time. The bank's time is similarly being wasted, which undermines its profitability. And the cause of all this aggravation and lost time is a lack of empathy for the customer.

If a duck bites you once, you barely feel it. But if a duck bites you repeatedly in the same spot, it's going to hurt. Not long after the problems with the misprinted checks and the online passwords, the man tries to change the mailing address for just one of his 17 accounts—but the bank mistakenly changes the addresses for all of them. But these mistakes are not a deal breaker for the customer, because he still has a great relationship with his personal banker. He knows he can pick up the phone and call his ally in the organization.

"The addresses were screwed up again, Paul, and I'm pissed off about it."

"I'm really sorry, Mr. Jones, and I promise to take care of the problem for you. I will make sure that this never happens again."

The lack of empathy that caused the problem is not only disappointing to the customer—it's also bad for the company's bottom line. "For all the inconvenience we put you through, I'm going to waive your bank fees this month," the representative says. The company's time and money is wasted as the employee spends hours fixing a problem that shouldn't have occurred in the first place.

And then the employee's manager asks him, "How come you're not out there getting me some new accounts?"

In any situation, consequences like this are the rotten fruit borne by a blatant lack of empathy—the problems that thoughtlessness causes for other people. And when those people are your customers, your business is in trouble.

## Breaking Up Is Hard to Do

Now the business is losing customers and trying to replace the accounts it's lost. There's not enough business coming through the door. Revenues are down. The remaining salespeople are forced to go out cold calling. The warm environment of referrals has frozen over. Conversion rates won't be as high, and the salespeople face an additional disadvantage when competing for customers against an incumbent business. In a tie, the incumbent will always win. Maybe it's inertia or just the customer preferring the devil he knows, but it's always harder to yank a customer away from a business where he's sitting comfortably at Level Two or Level Three. Ironically, it's only with some powerhouse, empathy-based USP that any company will succeed in converting an incumbent's customer—but if the organization had been offering that empathy all along, it probably wouldn't have lost the customer that it's now trying to replace.

The company that's losing business soon finds itself with too much capacity. It has more employees than deals, and has to start laying people off. And what's really causing the layoffs? Superficially at least, the backroom is at fault, with its lack of empathy for the salesperson and the customer. But ultimately it's up to the business owner to create an empathetic environment. That's how you keep customers soaring at Level Three, and the referrals pouring through your door. It all starts with empathy.

# Chapter Five

# *The Empathy Effect and Company Culture*

I n 1995, when the epiphany popped and I resolved to re-brand Majestic Mortgage with empathy-based USPs, I didn't know what a company culture was. I had never thought about it before. As a small broker with no big corporate experience, I was happy running my business my own way. But some things were happening in my company that were creating a huge conflict with my personal values. I discovered that certain loan officers were bending the rules for their own gain. Ego kills empathy, and when you're only looking out for yourself, other people suffer. In this case, they were my customers, vendors, employees, and myself.

But the root of the problem was that we were a company without an identity. Lacking a defined marketing platform and a clear set of company values, we bounced haphazardly between the extremes of trying to offer good customer service and bargain-basement interest rates. The staff didn't know who we were, what we stood for, where we were going, or how we would get there.

Eventually I would learn that every company has a culture, good or bad, whether the owners realize it or not. After I decided to distinguish Majestic Mortgage with empathy-based services, our culture began to evolve along empathetic lines. It came together piece by piece, through intuition more than by premeditation. And it wasn't until a couple of years later, when the culture had become well formed, that

I could look back and realize we had been building one.

Like many entrepreneurs, I had a rebellious, maverick mindset. I thought I could play the game better than any of the big shots could. Even the idea of packaging a business plan seemed too formal and sterile for me. Someone suggested that I use business-plan software, but I think people put too much stock into such formulas. The problem is that rote computer programs don't inspire soul searching. You never go deep inside and ask yourself, "What is it that I want my customer to experience? How do I want my employees to see this company, to look at each other and at me? What is acceptable in my company, and what is not?" As author Robert C. Dunwoody points out in his book, *You Can Have it All!*, you have to start with a vision before you can formulate a plan. I wanted to establish some parameters so that even if we occasionally wandered, ultimately we would stay on course. My goal was to provide the customers and the employees with a great experience, and I also wanted one for myself, too.

Even as our Empathy Effect culture began to take shape, our only way to find new people was to hire them from other mortgage companies. It quickly became apparent that these pilfered recruits would not be good matches for us. Many of them had picked up bad habits at their old companies, and their attitudes weren't geared toward empathetic customer service. It didn't work to try and tell them, "We do things differently around here." Some new hires fought our company culture, creating stress for everyone involved.

One employee was always saying, "At Chase, we used to do it this way...." So finally I took her outside, without wearing coats, to look at the sign on our building. Shivering because the temperature was three degrees, I asked her to slowly read the sign.

"It says 'Majestic Mortgage.'"

"It doesn't say 'Chase,' right? Could you even make 'Chase' out of the letters in 'Majestic Mortgage'?"

"No."

"Then that's the last I want to hear about how it was done at Chase."

To build a team of empathy-based loan officers we would mostly have to train new recruits, young people straight out of college or with just a little bit of work experience. Before we could begin assimilating industry veterans into our company culture, we would first have to build a core group of people who believed in our vision. Only then could we add outsiders, who would be in the minority and have to adapt to our way of doing things.

I knew that our customers worked hard to become homeowners, saving money for years, making sacrifices. Closing on a home loan is a momentous event in their lives, and I wanted the transactions to go smoothly and the customers to have great experiences. To kick-start the circular motion of The Empathy Effect, I started sending surveys to every customer who closed a loan with us—a practice we continue to this day. The questionnaire asks what the customer liked and didn't like about his or her experience with Majestic Mortgage. I thought people might be more candid if the survey looked like it could have come from a research firm rather than from us, so we designed the card with an anonymous post office box as the return address.

## Here Comes The Empathy Effect

I want to know exactly what's going on in my company, so I'm always the first one to read the surveys. One Friday evening I'm getting ready to leave the office for the wedding of an employee, Jodi Farmer, when the latest batch of responses lands on my desk.

"I'll just read these before I go," I tell myself, slicing open the first envelope.

In response to the question, "What would you recommend that we improve?", the first card reads, "Everything was great, if only we could have received our closing figures earlier. We had to rush to get a cashiers check at the last minute, and it was a little bit stressful. But other than that, we would still recommend you."

I make a mental note of the comment, and then open the second envelope. This one is from another customer, about a different loan officer, but it says almost exactly the same thing. The customer's experience was great for the most part, "But we wish we would have received the closing figures earlier. We got them at nine o'clock in the morning for an eleven o'clock closing, and had to scramble to get the cashiers check on time. We would suggest that you do something to improve that part of the process."

Ouch, two in a row. I open the third envelope. And I'll be damned if it doesn't say the same thing as the first two. That's three customers in a row complaining about the stress we caused them by not being more empathetic to their situations.

The easy solution would be to simply say, "Oh, well, last-minute closing figures are the norm in this industry, and there's nothing I can do about it." But I can't just sit back and accept the status quo. The last thing I want to do is create stress for my customers. I'm feeling ashamed, like I've done something morally wrong. The problem is still vexing my mind as I pack up and go home to change for the wedding. Renee is at the house with our kids, and she'll join me later at the reception.

I drive alone to a neighborhood church that sits among the houses on a quiet residential street in Winnetka, one of Chicago's affluent North Shore suburbs. As I walk in and find a seat in the pews, the quandary of the closing figures is still wearing on my mind. How am I going to solve this problem?

The wedding starts. A young woman from The Chicago Symphony Orchestra begins singing, accompanied by a man playing piano. Right on cue, a couple of little kids come down the aisle, dropping rose petals on the silk floor runner. The ceremony is proceeding flawlessly. The groom appears through a side door, followed by the bridesmaids. Then, to the chords of "Here Comes the Bride," Jodi walks down the aisle at exactly the right moment. Her dad lifts her veil and shakes the groom's hand. It's a perfectly executed performance.

I'm thinking to myself, "How can these people orchestrate this wedding so well, but we can't pull off a simple thing like getting customers their documents sooner before the closing?"

And then the answer hits me like a line drive: "Wait a minute—they practiced the wedding the night before, *at the rehearsal!*" Everyone walked through their roles in advance. The singer had probably been practicing for weeks.

As I sat there in the little church, it finally dawned on me that we were sending our customers to the single largest transaction of their lives without rehearsing it beforehand. As a company we had not stopped to think about what the customers' experience would be like under the conditions that we were creating for them. There was no empathy in that. At the last minute, we were telling customers to go get a cashiers check for a huge amount of money—a figure that we couldn't explain to them until the closing had already started and the atmosphere had become heated and stressful. The pressure during a closing is intense. You're in a frantic race to resolve any disagreements and sign all the documents within the allotted time, as if an hourglass has been flipped over and the sand is quickly running out. How would I feel if I were the customer in that situation, and my mortgage company hadn't given me the right numbers until the last minute? Not too happy. We weren't the only company dropping this fly ball—no one in the mortgage business rehearsed closings or provided early figures. But I wanted to reduce the customer's stress and give them a better experience. So just as the wedding party had practiced the ceremony, I determined to make it company policy that we would rehearse every closing with the customer three business days before the transaction itself.

## Another Fateful Occurrence

Like other signs I've received over the years, the epiphany about the closing rehearsal came about through a bizarre set of coincidental circumstances. If I hadn't read three customer surveys with the same complaint right before leaving for the wedding, or if Renee and the kids had been with me at the church, taking my attention, I probably would have missed the opportunity to discover what would become one of my company's most important empathy-based USPs, and the catalyst for our change to an Empathy Effect culture.

## Breaking the Inertia Block

In direct response to customer suggestions that we furnish the closing numbers earlier in the process, we worked our rear ends off to
give the title company the figures three days before the closing. But
we soon heard them blaming us for their own procrastination. When
the customer would call asking for the figures—already worried about
having enough time to procure the cashiers check, which is why
they're calling—the title company would tell them, "Sorry, but your
mortgage company hasn't given us those numbers yet." The aggra-
vated customer would call us next, asking why we were late with this
crucial information. Of course we knew that we had sent the figures
to the title company days before, and that they just hadn't prepared
the HUD-1 closing statement yet. They wouldn't get to it until they
absolutely had to, at the last minute. That was how their system oper-
ated. Stuck in inertia, the title companies weren't going to change. If
we wanted to improve our customers' experience, we would have to
do something differently ourselves.

One of the biggest obstacles to improving a company's culture is
that the owners lack the opportunity—or the nerve—to challenge the
system. The whole operation bogs down, constrained by the idea that,
"This is the way it's always been done."

Making a move that's unheard of in the mortgage business, we
bought the software to add the HUD-1 closing statement to our own
system, and started compiling the forms ourselves. The HUD-1 lists
and itemizes all the numbers the borrower will need to know—the
loan amount, the size of the down payment, closing costs and fees,
whether escrows are being waived, etc. Most important, it tells the
customer the amount of the cashiers check he'll need at the closing,
so he can obtain it at a more relaxed pace, before pressure builds in
the final hours before the transaction.

I knew we didn't have to take this extra step. We could have just
told ourselves, "Well, it's really the title company's job to buy that
software and provide the closing figures, not ours,"—which appears
to be the attitude of most mortgage companies. But I wanted to im-

prove our customers' experience, and show them some empathy. By practicing The Empathy Effect, we would benefit our customers and ourselves. Three days before the closing we would give the customer a copy of their statement, and then over the telephone walk them down the list of figures, explaining each item and how much it would cost. These are the final numbers, and there won't be any changes or surprises about them at the last minute.

By rehearsing the transaction, we would not only vanquish the customer's 11th-hour scramble for a cashiers check and other stresses that plague unrehearsed closings, but we would also prevent much of the anxiety that people might otherwise experience in the days leading up to the closing. Having rehearsed this huge transaction, the customer doesn't feel anxious or intimidated. They know what to expect. The process has been demystified. And we're the heroes. As measured by our surveys, customer satisfaction shot way up after we started providing the rehearsals and early figures.

Despite the success of these empathy-based USPs, I can't think of a single other mortgage company or competitor that now offers anything similar. The idea of a closing rehearsal is difficult for the industry to accept because it's a huge shift away from the established norm. There's too much inertia blocking such a radical change. But the evolution isn't difficult for a company that wants to embrace The Empathy Effect. To reliably deliver empathy-based services, you need an empathetic company culture. Unfortunately, the industry's usual idea of "The Golden Rule" is, "I have the gold, so I make the rules." For customers of these companies, the tacit message seems to be, "You can't close the loan without me, so you'll just have to wait, and the title company will have to deal with it, too." It's easy to see why this ego-driven, antipathetic approach kills a company's long-term profitability.

## Stress Drops, Satisfaction Rises

A business owner seeking to create an Empathy Effect company culture must be willing to challenge the status quo with his or her own staff. Sometimes the first step of The Empathy Effect doesn't look like empathy at all.

When I initially proposed the rehearsal to my closing department, they said, "Tom, you're crazy. We don't have time to rehearse with every customer!"

"I know how you feel," I said. "But let's just try it for 30 days and see what happens. By putting forth this effort upfront, I think you'll save yourself a lot of time and aggravation in the long run."

I knew my employees were burning energy trying to fix glitches in the pressure-cooker environment of the closing, while attorneys paced the floor, Realtors were anxious to leave for their next appointments—and worst of all, our customers were becoming stressed out and upset.

"By rehearsing the closing with accurate numbers, you'll be under less pressure, so you'll make fewer mistakes," I told my staff. "And when you do make a mistake, it won't happen in the heat of the battle. You'll have time to fix it."

Maybe it was because I lacked traditional mortgage-company experience that I wrote my own rule book. But I still faced the risk that my entire closing department might walk out if I made them start rehearsing every transaction with the customers. The irony is that today, the closing staff probably stays together *because* of the rehearsals and the lower stress they allow, not in spite of them. Who knows, maybe my closing department would walk out if I were to stop offering this empathy-based USP, which benefits them as much as it does the customers.

A shift was underway for our company culture, a movement toward empathy. I didn't know for sure that it would work, but I had a good feeling about it. Despite some initial reservations, the closing staff indulged my request, and pretty soon they started to feel The Empathy Effect as their stress levels dropped and their job satisfaction went way up. If something goes wrong—a customer changes a loan amount, decides to waive escrows, has less earnest money than he thought, or says, "I forgot to tell you, I had the builder add a Jacuzzi in the backyard," increasing the home's purchase price by $5,000—the closing department would now have three days to fix the problem, rather than just a few hours or minutes. At unrehearsed closings, common vicissitudes turn into nightmares. The deal is wrong. The numbers don't match up. By rehearsing the transaction and providing accurate documentation three days early, we're eliminating the reactive, stressful workload that last-minute changes dump on people. It's better for us and for our customers. By making the experience easier for everyone, The Empathy Effect also touches our lead sources, the Realtors and homebuilders. The Empathy Effect reverberates far into the future, in this context spurring repeat business and referrals, which in turn each create their own Empathy Effects, and so on.

Psychologists say people are motivated more by fear of pain than by the possibility of reward. What we found was that customers don't mind investing time upfront in order to avoid hassles later. As consumers, they've experienced enough unpleasant transactions in their lives, and for purchases far less important than their homes. People have to sign lots of documents at the closing, but going into it what they really want to know is, "Am I getting the right interest rate? Are my closing costs correct, and how much money should I bring? What will my loan amount be, and when is my first payment due?"

With all of these questions answered three days in advance, instead of during the frenzy of the transaction, we found the customer sitting relaxed at the closing table. "I'm okay with this. I've already gone through all the numbers with my loan officer. Just give me the stack of documents to sign."

First-time homebuyers don't always recognize the value of this empathy-based USP, because they've never had a different closing experience for comparison. But customers who've closed loans elsewhere and then come to Majestic really appreciate the difference. With people moving up to bigger and better houses, and taking advantage of low interest rates to refinance existing home loans, they might experience several closings over a period of ten years. We've had situations where someone closes their first and second loans with us, not realizing that our rehearsal and Empathy Effect culture are exceptions to the industry's rule. They try a different company for their third closing, and have a terrible experience. For their fourth closing they come back to us, saying, "Tom, we promise we'll never leave you again. You don't give yourself enough credit that this is a really hard thing to do."

When we first started the closing rehearsals, I was still a loan officer myself, besides running the company. I remember the first time I walked a customer through the three-day-early figures. This particular client was a high-net-worth business owner, and slightly eccentric. He was so smart that he could quote the ticker symbols and opening and closing prices for 40 different bellwether stocks, and yet he couldn't find his car keys. He bought a Lincoln Continental with a keyless entry, just so he could leave his keys in the car and remember the code instead.

"You can get whatever loan amount you want," I told him when he first came to see me for a mortgage. "How much would you like?"

"Just give me $234,000," he said.

At the time, $240,000 was the maximum conforming loan amount that Fannie Mae and Freddie Mac would fund through their purchases of mortgages on the secondary market, which are then bundled as mortgage-backed securities and sold to investors.

A couple weeks later when we rehearsed the closing, my client seemed to have forgotten the loan amount we had agreed on.

"No, $234,000 won't be enough," he said. "I'll have to bring too large a check to the closing to cover the difference. I wanted to take the loan all the way to $240,000."

My notes showed that we had agreed to $234,000, but I couldn't very well argue with my customer. So I just smiled and said, "No problem." I knew I had three days to fix the discrepancy with my underwriting department. It would all be done behind the scenes.

Three days later when the deal went to closing, the customer, the attorney, the Realtor and the title-company rep all looked at each other and said, "Wow, that's the smoothest transaction we've ever seen!" They didn't realize that we had spent a few extra hours fixing the problem after the customer had changed his mind.

Compared to responding in last-minute-crisis mode, this approach was low stress, manageable and effective. And its origin was empathy. The USP had its genesis when we started asking customers their likes and dislikes about their experience of closing home loans with us. The surveys had set the empathy wheel in motion, and now it was picking up speed.

## Empathy for Vendors?

With the closing rehearsals humming along, we really began to shine in our customers' eyes. No other mortgage companies were doing it. The customers saw their own experiences improve dramatically, and also watched The Empathy Effect sweep over the other people involved in the closing. Rave reviews started pouring in from customers, title companies and lawyers, and repeat business and referrals soon followed. Before receiving their stacks of work in the morning, title-company employees would lobby to get our files. They knew the closing would be infinitely smoother with us than with XYZ mortgage company. The closing rehearsal also makes life easier for the attorneys. "If it's a Majestic closing," they've told us, "it's a piece of cake."

As our Empathy Effect culture took shape, capacities went up, stress went down, and client loyalty shot through the roof. The closing rehearsal helped our loan officers attract more customers, almost exclusively through referrals. Profitability increased because we no longer had to offer discounts to resolve disputes and delays at the closing table. Realtors and homebuilders could see the great experience our mutual customers were having. Naturally these real estate professionals become upset when closings are delayed or not funded, so the promise of a smooth transaction rapidly multiplied our base of lead sources.

At Majestic Mortgage, our Empathy Effect culture goes beyond understanding the customer's needs. We also try to empathize with the situations of the other parties participating in the real estate transaction. For the title companies, business goes in cycles of feast or famine. During a feast period, they have to hire more people to handle the heavier workload, and often those new people lack experience. And that can cause problems for the title companies and for us. In the mortgage business we use net drafting, or net wiring, of funds. If I had $935 coming back to me in a $100,000 transaction, I would only send $99,065 to the closing table, in a net draft. The title company would have to balance the numbers on their end. Instead of waiting for them to send me back a check for $935, I would deduct that amount from the size of the homebuyer's loan amount, and then not have to deal with it later.

At least that's how we did it before realizing that the title company's less-experienced new hires were having a hard time reconciling the numbers. They couldn't figure out where the numbers were supposed to go, couldn't add them up. And, unfortunately for everyone involved, this disconnect was happening at the worst possible time, during the stress of the closing. So finally we told ourselves, "This isn't worth the aggravation. Let's just give them the entire amount of $100,000, and then let them send us back a check for $935. If they don't, then we'll fight that battle—but not in the heat of the action during the closing."

When we bought the software to generate the HUD-1, we started sending a copy of each form to the title company. Rather than confusing them with a set of written instructions that would probably create mismatched results, we took a visual approach instead: "Make your closing statement look just like this one." All they had to do was fill in the numbers. And lo and behold, the old problems started to disappear. The transactions became smooth and harmonious, with no disconnections or confusion. All of a sudden, closings weren't so stressful anymore.

Any company will benefit by showing empathy to its vendors. I know it's not my job to spend time researching and understanding the needs of someone I'm paying to perform a service, but I usually do it anyway. When I show empathy to my vendors, they soak it up and radiate it back to me. Having empathy for vendors doesn't mean excusing poor performance or incompetence. Not by a long shot. That would only create a negative result for everyone involved, which runs contrary to the mutually beneficial nature of The Empathy Effect.

Showing empathy to vendors means understanding their motivations and point of view, not feeling sorry for them. Once you've put trial and error behind you and find good, reliable vendors, it's to your mutual benefit to show them some empathy.

As someone who had opened a mortgage company without ever having taken a loan application before, I had heard the disparaging comments: "How's he going to survive in this business?" the naysayers would snipe. "He doesn't understand it!"

So I had to learn the business from the back forward—backwards thinking. Part of that education came from having empathy for the underwriters, the outside contractors who assess a loan applicant's risk based on their credit history and overall financial strength. (Today, the digital revolution has automated the underwriting process and brought it in-house, but during the late 1980s we were still hiring out the service.) To learn my business from the back to the front, I had to understand what the underwriters were up against. Back when I had sold real estate and was recommending mortgage companies to my customers, the mortgage people would never explain to me how underwriting worked. They probably didn't understand it themselves. Underwriting was like a secret locked in a black box. Later when I opened my own mortgage company, underwriters were still a big mystery to me. Most small brokers seemed to think that underwriting was something you shouldn't even try to understand. Fannie Mae and Freddie Mac were like the Great and Powerful Oz. As was often the case when I first entered this new business of consumer home loans, the complacency that mortgage people showed about not understanding underwriters didn't make any sense to me. "It can't be like that," I told myself. "There have got to be some tangible rules here."

If underwriters had to follow the Fannie Mae and Freddie Mac guidelines, then I would learn those rules myself and demystify the black box. I would practice The Empathy Effect with these vendors, for our mutual benefit.

Just as we had bought the software to generate our own HUD-1 statements and make life easier for the title companies, ourselves and our customers, now we practiced The Empathy Effect for underwriters by purchasing and studying the Fannie Mae and Freddie Mac guidelines. I bought all four manuals, for $1,600. I only needed half of one manual, but to get it I had to purchase the entire set.

I really wanted to understand what the underwriters were dealing with, so I dug into the manual. Once I had learned the guidelines that govern my vendor's practices, I became an active participant in their decisions, rather than just a passive observer. When an underwriter would tell me that there was a rule for why I had to do something a certain way, now I could reply, "Really, where does it say that in the manual? In section 2.5? Well, maybe I'm wrong, but I don't think that's what it's saying here. It says I can use the borrower's income as long as it's 36 months in nature...."

The underwriters were amazed that a mortgage guy had taken the time to read the guidelines and understand their business. It was something they'd probably never experienced before.

"Wow, okay, well.... Maybe I've got an outdated manual...."

Not wanting to embarrass them, I'd say, "Maybe my book is outdated," even though I knew I had the most up-to-date version.

By the end of our conversation, the underwriter would realize that I had the correct information.

"Well, in that case, I'll go ahead and approve this loan."

By taking the extra effort to practice The Empathy Effect for the vendor, we improved the outcome for everyone involved.

Later on, Merchants Bank in Indianapolis was buying about 80% of the home loans my company originated, and I got to know the head underwriter there well. At the time, her name was Maryann Green.

When I visited the bank staff for a social function, she asked me, "Tom, how'd you get all your underwriting experience?"

"Maryann, I've never underwritten a loan in my life."

Her eyes widened in disbelief. "What? You've got to be kidding me! You seem to really understand what we're going through."

Because I knew what Maryann was up against with the agencies, I became a better client to her, which probably meant that she gave me the benefit of the doubt more often than not. Understanding vendors will save any business owner pain, trials and tribulations.

The rep at Merchants Bank, a guy named Rod Hoenschel, said to me, "Tom, you know what makes you a great client? You're as worried about us as we are about you."

I began to see how The Empathy Effect for vendors fits into the big picture of my company's culture. If I didn't bother to learn the issues facing my underwriters, and my loans ultimately put them out of business, my indifference would not only hurt them, but I would also have the burden of finding a new vendor and establishing another relationship. What I realized was that most conflicts are rooted in misunderstandings, and that misunderstandings are not just innocent mistakes. They're often caused by a stubborn refusal to understand or consider another person's point of view. In other words, misunderstandings are caused by a lack of empathy. The conflicts that result are a waste of everyone's time and energy—and not coincidentally, a drain on profitability, too. Antipathy and misunderstandings can cause grudges that last for years, heaping negativity on top of negativity, like paying usurious interest on a debt. The Empathy Effect, on the other hand, promotes understanding and cooperation, reducing conflict or eliminating it altogether. Empathy creates something positive with everyone's time, spinning the hours into gold.

The more vendors that a company uses, the more its survival depends on practicing The Empathy Effect. Empathy keeps the organism healthy. If one part of it becomes infected with antipathy, the entire company is threatened. The bad cells can't be allowed to spread.

Consider the vast array of vendors that contract with the automobile industry. Thousands of companies provide parts to help build cars, from the oil filter and the tires to the CD player in the dash. General Motors orchestrates an immense system of vendors and suppliers, and makes sure that standards are followed. After all, if something goes wrong with a car, it's GM's reputation that suffers, not that of its vendors. The consumer might not even realize that a different company supplied the part that blew out. And then GM gets stuck with the recalls, lawsuits, bad publicity and tarnished brands. The symbiotic relationship between clients and vendors will always run smoother with the mutually advantageous touch of The Empathy Effect.

Wal-Mart has been accused of bullying its vendors, and at first glance, the accusations might appear true. Suppliers to the world's largest retailer are pushed to keep prices down by manufacturing goods more efficiently, and are held to the strictest standards in this business for keeping store shelves stocked at all times. Wal-Mart understands what consumers want more than its suppliers do, even going so far as to determine the goods that will be produced in the first place. Some might call it intimidation, but in reality Wal-Mart is saving the vendor with these stringent rules, guaranteeing that the smaller player will continue doing business with the biggest retailer on the planet. In essence, Wal-Mart is telling its suppliers, "If you can't perform and warehouse this merchandise for me, and get it here on time, and at the right price, then you're not qualified to be a Wal-Mart vendor."

Being a Wal-Mart vendor is a privileged position. If Wal-Mart doesn't press its suppliers to perform, consumers will suffer, and then so will the vendors. Just about everyone involved benefits—the millions of consumers who enjoy lower prices and a reliable supply of merchandise, the company and its shareholders, and the vendors. Unfortunately in the case of Wal-Mart, the USP of bargain-basement prices becomes a missing link in the empathy chain. Its employees are forbidden from unionizing and earn only about $9 per hour, and many can't afford to pay for health insurance premiums.

## Empathy and the Three-Way Balancing Act

For a company culture to deliver The Empathy Effect, the owners or managers have to maintain a three-way balancing act—taking care of the customers, the employees and the profit. It's a difficult balance, especially when you first try to turn a company culture in a new direction. For companies suffocating under apathetic or antipathetic cultures, the move toward empathy can seem like trying to dislodge a 20-ton boulder that's half sunk in mud. But once the initial struggle has passed, The Empathy Effect begins to wash away the negative grime. The balancing act of customers, profit and employees becomes natural and systemic.

First and foremost, every business has to take care of its customers, whether the obligation is price, value or the overall experience. Otherwise, the customer won't come back. But the balancing act also requires profit. As a business owner you have to maintain a profit for your personally, privately held company, so the endeavor is worth the spilling of your blood, sweat and tears. Without profit to cover the risk, you're going to get out. On the other hand, if you start making too much money from your customers, you'll lose them. And naturally you have to take care of your employees, too. It's a delicate balance.

## Empathy Requires Adaptive Thinking

Having empathy for the customer means understanding what they really want. Besides coming right out and asking them, you can spot clues about your customers' preferences by looking around, and anticipating. If your customer is a consumer, remember that you're one, too. Think about what you would want for yourself. People who serve consumers tend to forget their own perspectives as consumers. They stick their heads in the sand and say, "No, that doesn't apply here." But it does. And even if your customer is not a consumer but another business, it's important to keep an eye on broader trends that might influence your customer's buying decisions.

Practicing The Empathy Effect with customers means remembering that times change. Industries fail because they don't look up and see what's happening today. To their detriment, some companies fail to heed the messages of emerging trends, relying instead on obsolete assumptions and processes.

Most consumers today are in families where both spouses are working. Even when just one spouse works, parents find themselves running from place to place to place. Amid the helter-skelter of this mad-dash lifestyle, consumers want great experiences for their money. They're looking to escape stress. Advice on stress reduction permeates the media, with endless books, magazine articles and talk shows devoted to the subject.

Companies that help consumers escape stress are meeting the demands of our times, and selling The Empathy Effect. Higher-end hotels understand this very well. When people frazzled from the rat race go on vacation or just spend a night out, they're willing to pay good money to be taken care of. The parallel trends of rising affluence and increasingly stressful lifestyles have fed the popularity of spas and "wellness centers," which are becoming standard in most luxury hotels. For guests looking to unwind after stressful business meetings or just pamper themselves on vacation, hotel spas demonstrate empathy by providing tranquility amid the chaos.

For the premiums they charge, luxury hotels and spas are under pressure to deliver an empathetic experience. But even a mass-market service like a drive-through restaurant can create The Empathy Effect by adapting to consumers' changing needs and reducing their stress.

Here in the Chicago area, a fast-food chain called Portillo's serves hot dogs, hamburgers, Italian beef sandwiches, salads and more. At lunchtime recently, there were 23 cars ahead of me in the drive-through line. But Portillo's' efficient, empathetic system slid me through and put hot food in my hands in only four minutes. When I first approached the restaurant and saw the long queue of cars, I didn't turn away because I felt confident that it would move quickly. Employees were running all over the place—two kids taking orders, another accepting the customers' money, other employees hustling bags of food out to the cars before they even reached the pick-up windows. I might be the seventh car in line, and they're running my order out to me. Portillo's knows why I'm going to a drive-through in the first place: I want my food fast, and I don't want to leave my car. They're practicing The Empathy Effect by addressing the changing needs of the American consumer, something that McDonald's has been chasing and stumbling after in catch-up mode for years.

## What Comes First, Profit or Profit Sharing?

Even when you're taking care of the customer and the profit, if you don't have adequate funds to properly reward your employees, then the first two spinning plates crash to the floor. You need enough money to keep pace with the times and compensate your people the right way. Otherwise you'll have a revolving door, and constant employee turnover rots away at customer service and profits. Mistakes lead to discounting, draining the bottom line. Pretty soon you're telling yourself, "This doesn't make any sense. Why am I doing this?"

But while underpaying employees kills The Empathy Effect, so does paying them too much. You might have great people and find yourself giving away the store to them. If your employees start earning more money than you do, and you're still taking care of the customer, at year's end you might think, "Wait a minute: I've got a million dollars tied up in my company, and I've made $10,000 in profit. That's just stupid." In this type of lop-sided scenario, you wind up defeating yourself, the employee and the customer.

I learned that when building a company culture, it's important to find the right essence match in your employees. Money-hungry hires who just want the biggest dollars and are going to burn through the company will ultimately destroy it. The type of employee who goes to the highest bidder will never stay in one organization for long. If someone says, "I need a bigger piece," and you give them a hefty raise that you really can't afford, your empathy is out of balance and will eventually cause your business to fail. Decisions on where to draw the empathy line have to be made according to how they affect the larger picture for everyone involved, which is a true Empathy Effect.

Before my company culture shifted toward empathy, we weren't making any profit. I found myself pondering a conundrum: *What comes first, profit or profit sharing?*

For my company, profit sharing preceded profit. I initially started a profit-sharing program because I thought the gesture would make my staff feel better. It wasn't a foregone conclusion that the program would increase my company's profits, and I don't think I even expected it to. But after the program got underway, I felt a greater purpose and responsibility to create profit for the company and the employees. The program provided a huge incentive for employees to cut costs, streamline processes, run the company more efficiently and continually find new ways to improve the customer's experience. The employees now had a financial stake in the outcome. And true to the circular nature of The Empathy Effect, as the company's profits increased, my personal income rose with the tide.

In an empathetic company culture, taking care of employees and maintaining profits become one and the same. When profits are shared, motivated employees push for more profit, and more profit creates motivated employees. Besides helping make my company profitable, profit sharing also shut down the revolving door. Employee loyalty and retention shot straight up.

Just as we ask ourselves what's important to the customer, we also have to answer the question, "What does the employee really want?" Are they only looking for the most possible pay, even if it means toiling in an environment that's heated with stress and antipathy? No, people don't want that. They would rather work someplace where they can feel like family. People want respect, and to be recognized for their work. And there's no better way to make employees feel appreciated than to let them share in the company's profits. Publicly traded companies use stock options. "If this company does well, I can make a lot of money." When the stock price goes higher, employee fortunes climb with it—an empathetic process and a strong retention tool.

Knowing that employee turnover causes problems for customers, I had to create a program for retaining my staff. The old days of pension plans and cradle-to-the-grave job security at companies like GM had mostly disappeared in America, amid downsizing, outsourcing and factories moving to Third World countries to satisfy demand for return on investment from wealthy shareholders. As the owner of a small company, I had to compete with the majors for the best employees in the labor pool. Again it came back to the question, "What is it that the employee really wants?" They want camaraderie with their peers, working for a fair company that has vision and potential, a company that shares profits so that the employee's hard work is rewarded, and not exploited for someone else's benefit. Most people aren't going to sell out the values that are important to them just for a little more money.

I distribute bonuses to my staff every year at our summer profit-sharing party. In 2003, I gave $365,000 in profit-sharing checks to my staff of 59 people (not including my top two executives and myself). It was a great feeling—for the employees, and believe it or not, maybe even more so for me. I could look at a kid who had just started with us the year before, fresh out of college, and give her a check for $8,800. It was like she had died and gone to heaven. Nothing gives me more satisfaction than knowing that I'm helping put people on paths of life faster than they could have by working anywhere else, including at the big corporations. One young lady on our staff is 23 years old, and she wants to buy her first house. She can see that the profit-sharing program is bringing that dream within range of becoming a reality, and the checks are taking leaps and bounds toward helping her save for the down payment.

We decided to have just a couple of rules for the profit-sharing bonuses: First, the employee has to have read a book selected by the company, and to provide a report on it at the profit-sharing party—another way to foster our consistent company culture. One of the titles was *Who Moved My Cheese?*, Spencer Johnson's simple but brilliant take on adapting to change. The other rule is that the employee has to spend the money on something he or she wouldn't ordinarily buy.

Pretty soon we started hearing comments like, "Our family had a wonderful experience at Disney World," or, "See that dining room set over there? That was from my profit sharing for 1998—1999."

With their share of the profits, the employees started buying vacations and toys that they probably never would have experienced otherwise—new decks on their houses, motorcycles, wave runners. Don't misunderstand my aim here: It's not about promoting materialism. Rather, it's about building memories, what my friend and mentor Todd Duncan calls "Majestic Moments." As our mission statement would later sum up, we were striving to create "an experience for our customers and our employees that is second to none." With the insistence that employees treat themselves with their profit-sharing money, we were building a culture where they would say, "Not only is this a great place to work, but look at all the memories the company has created for my family." The top-producer trips to Hawaii have had the same effect.

## Empathy Promotes Teamwork and Profit

Teamwork is a great idea in theory, but it won't happen if people are wasting their time on petty rivalries and don't respect each other. Teamwork requires an environment that fosters empathy, particularly as the company grows larger.

When I first resolved to start a profit-sharing program, I wasn't sure how to divide up the money. Should every employee get an equal share? Would that be fair and equitable? Or should merit determine the size of the slice?

I would eventually decide to use a peer-voting process, where each employee anonymously rates the others on a numerical scale. We would tally up the numbers and determine each person's average score, and then write a check for an amount that correlates to that number. The peer-rating system would further inspire each employee to give his or her best. Part of the vision involved with The Empathy Effect, especially for managers, is to push people to reach their full potential as employees and as human beings—or at least to firmly nudge them. Compare that to the antipathetic alternative of deliberately squashing another person's potential, which happens all the time in company cultures poisoned by ego and politics.

The voting system would make our profit-sharing allotments fair and equitable. It ensured that great performers would receive a larger reward than mediocre performers, while also motivating the medio-cre performers to improve. Ironically, it's sometimes the least greedy employees who end up making the most money, because in a profit-sharing scenario their conscientious work ethic naturally comes back to reward them.

Peer voting also increased harmony between departments, and made personnel crossovers smoother whenever the need would arise. People knew they were being evaluated by everyone else in the company, so they started making more of an effort to get along and work well together. Employees showed each other greater respect, and greater empathy. People in the operations department, what I call the "backroom," realized that if they created terrific experiences for the customers, then the loan officers wouldn't have to offer discounts to compensate for mistakes. And no discounts means there are more profits to be shared.

Retaining the best employees also requires giving them room to grow and advance. With empathy it's easy to imagine the feeling of pride and accomplishment that a person feels when their hard work earns them a promotion. A company environment that encourages devotion in employees is also one where they can follow their talents and interests. Sometimes the freedom to make a sideways move into a different department that's a better fit can be as important to someone as the promotion that might come later. As John Maxwell says, "Learn to put people in the right places."

## An Atmosphere of Cooperation

A major culture change for my company occurred when we started allowing crossover between our sales and operations departments, whenever the employee's career and personal situations would call for it. Before the change, the operations department jealously guarded its people, and so did sales. They wouldn't let someone move from operations to sales, even when the sales department desperately needed more assistants. Conversely, when an otherwise strong employee didn't work out in sales, we had nowhere to move them, either. But as we modified our culture and people throughout the company began embracing our empathy vision, lateral movements started to happen between operations and sales and we soon found that empathy was growing between the former rival departments.

Fostering an atmosphere of cooperation and trust between the sales team and the operations department is crucial to the success of my company. In any organization, a sales person might romance a customer for six, seven months, even a year or two, depending on the buying cycle for the particular product. After all of that effort and time is invested, if the operations department lets the salesperson down and screws something up for his customer, then the salesperson will only get that one sale. Despite all the work the salesperson has put into acquiring the customer, the customer will never return. The backroom has to come through for the sales department so that sales can come through for them—the circular nature of The Empathy Effect. When the backroom fails the sales force, the salespeople will not only lose the customer, they might develop a bad reputation that prevents referrals. And once again, mistakes lead to discounting, undercutting profits for everyone in the company.

## Facing Up to Your Company Culture

Business owners who want to create The Empathy Effect should ask themselves: Is my company culture empathetic to the needs and motivations of other people, customers and employees alike? Or does it breed apathy and antipathy, which lead to a lack of profitability? One force or another will dominate your company culture. If there's no empathy, then apathy or antipathy will take its place. The slate is never blank.

To deliver The Empathy Effect consistently and reliably, an organization must have empathy ingrained into its culture. From the CEO to the receptionist, every member of the team has to have an empathetic heart.

# Chapter Six

# *The Power of Empathetic Leadership*

Before I re-branded my company with an empathy-based culture, my employees weren't sticking around for long. We had a revolving door spinning faster than at Macy's. Until I realized what a mistake it was to recruit employees from conventional mortgage companies that touted low rates and gave customers lousy service, I was hiring the wrong people. Maybe these mismatched hires wanted to stay at my company, but I didn't want to keep them.

By the time I realized that I was building a company culture based on providing "an experience to our customers and our employees that is second to none," I also saw that culture starts at the top and flows down. It's up to the business owner—with his or her words and actions—to set a productively empathetic example for the staff to follow.

Conversely, we've all seen antipathetic owners and managers. You know the type: Motivated only by self-interest, he's got his employees so overworked and stressed that they're hurtling towards burnout, sweating and scrambling to keep up—and then he yells at them for not being productive enough. This jerk has no idea how hard his people are working, and he doesn't respect them enough to care. Far from appreciating all of their efforts to keep his company running, the antipathetic manager demeans the employees in front of their co-workers. Tact is foreign to his nature. When something goes wrong, he prefers the convenience of finding one person to blame. From where Mr. Clueless stands, all of his employees' tasks and responsibilities seem simple enough. Quick in jumping to negative conclusions, he sees only the hasty generalization, the easy explanation of a complex situation or problem. He can't imagine all the intricate details and challenges involved for his employees. He has never stood in their shoes or performed their jobs, and has no understanding of what they face every day.

Clueless managers also tend to be the ones who quickly lose their patience and tempers with employees—different characteristics of the same lack of empathy. The antipathetic business owner regards personnel as expendable resources, cordwood to chuck and burn so he can power his own engine. He tries to sell his employees on the idea that long hours of work are more important than anything else in their lives, that leisure is strictly for the lazy, even as he spends half his time on vacation playing golf. Needless to say, this self-interested, ego-driven business owner does not share profits with his employees. He's as greedy as he is tactless. When his company manages to have a banner year, he gathers his staff to announce the news, but only gives them $10 movie passes as a reward. This leader has zero empathy. And it's poisoning his company.

Unless this character has a monopoly in his marketplace, running, let's say, the only window-repair company in town, his business won't last long. At best, he'll fall into a profit-draining cycle of continually losing his best employees and customers. When employees fear and resent the boss, they will try to hurt him in some way. Whether through apathy about their work, pilferage or grand embezzlement, disgruntled employees will find ways to undermine an antipathetic employer. In a decent job market, they'll just leave and get a better position somewhere else.

Consistently, about one in four of the antipathetic owner's new hires won't work out, often because of conflicts with him, and he'll fire them before three months to avoid paying unemployment compensation. Two other new hires will quit within the first year, disgusted by the owner and the hostile working environment he has created. Maybe one in four will be the superstars that he really needs on his team. These people are smart and talented, sometimes even more so than they reveal. They can see clearly that their employer's attitude is devoid of empathy. But this 25% of new hires might stick around for a few years anyway, because they're clever and resourceful enough to expand the parameters of their job descriptions to include new projects which they personally find challenging and rewarding. Mr. Clueless knows these A-list players are keeping his clients happy and making him money, so for a while at least, he stays out of their way. But cracks continue to spread through the foundation of his business. Before long the owner's antipathetic attitude will alienate even his top people. Mismatched employees and customers will come and go with the seasons, but the more damaging consequence of Mr. Clueless's lack of empathy is that once every three or four years, his best employees will leave him in a mass exodus. In his blindness, the self-interested manager has mistakenly come to believe that these people are his loyal lieutenants, even though he's been exploiting them all along. First one leaves, then another and another, and within a year all of the company's top talent has bolted. The bedrock of the company's day-to-day operations crumbles. And then the antipathetic owner has to try and rebuild.

With management as well as the rank-and-file in constant flux, the quality of the company's work is bound to decline—if it was ever any good in the first place. Tired of the discontinuity of dealing with a new employee every time, and fed up with rookies who can't deliver quality work and a great experience, customers will take their business elsewhere. Just as Mr. Clueless has no empathy for his employees, he doesn't understand the needs, motivations and everyday frustrations of his customers, either. He has never bothered to consider their point of view. Here's a guy who wants to run his own company, but he remains willfully oblivious to the sour experience he's giving his employees and his customers. Soon he'll find himself more in the business of interviewing applicants, training green hires and chasing new accounts than in providing his purported product or service. Along with the talent drain, profit is also bleeding from the company. The antipathetic business owner is constantly trying to stay ahead of disaster, like running across a series of rocks in the water and hoping that the jump to the next landing won't prove too far to reach. Sooner or later, he's going down. And his former top people will be prospering elsewhere.

## Misdirected Empathy?

I began to ponder what it means to practice The Empathy Effect as a manager. At one extreme there's Mr. Clueless, who doesn't know what his customers and employees want or need. But what's the opposite extreme of the oblivious, angry manager? Is it somebody who is so keenly aware of his employees' stresses, and feels their pain so sympathetically, that he excuses poor performance and lets standards slide? Would too much empathy be a bad thing?

What I eventually realized was that The Empathy Effect won't happen when a manager tolerates—and therefore encourages—sloppy work from his staff.

"Oh, well, it's okay if this order didn't go through.... I understand, don't worry about it...."

In that case, the manager is not practicing The Empathy Effect. By forgiving poor performance, he ends up hurting the employee, the customer and the company. A leader who lets his team fail because he's too lenient with the players is a bad leader. He's not keeping the end goal in mind.

## Giving Bitter Medicine

True empathy means looking out for the other person's best interests in the larger sense. And that might require you to seem a little tough at first. This is where it becomes more difficult for the empathetic manager, being firm with people you respect and admire. But the alternative could be misplaced empathy, which undoes The Empathy Effect.

Consider chemotherapy: What if an oncologist was more worried about his cancer patient's appearance than with battling the disease?

"This person is a movie star. What would happen to his career if I gave him chemotherapy and his hair fell out?"

The Empathy Effect supports the ultimate goal, not the immediate comfort of those involved. If the client wants to lose weight and get into shape, the personal trainer has to overlook short-term empathy and keep an eye on the final objective, even if he risks alienating his client in the short run.

He can't say, "Man, this guy is really blowing some steam here. Maybe I should back off."

If the trainer doesn't work the Olympic athlete hard enough, she's not going to win that gold medal. A competitor won't even make it to the Olympics without someone pushing her to win. For the leader, softness would cause failure. Misdirected empathy would defeat both the athlete and her trainer.

Big-picture empathy also affects how we raise our kids. She wants to be out with her friends until one o'clock in the morning. Superficially at least, there appears to be no empathy in this conversation.

"No way. Curfew is at 11:30, and you're going to be home by then."

"Oh, c'mon, Dad! You were a kid once before, too. Can't you relate? We're just going to be at Mary's house."

"No. Get yourself home by 11:30."

My daughter might think I'm being unsympathetic, but really I'm making an unpopular decision so that I can achieve The Empathy Effect on a larger scale. The ultimate goal is to protect my child and her best interests, not to give her immediate gratification with a decision that I know could threaten her safety and security.

How do you discipline a child and still maintain a cleanly drawn circle for The Empathy Effect? "Well, I really shouldn't yell at her...." Baloney, yell at her! We're teaching our daughter to be an adult. "Don't have bad manners in the restaurant." She might roll her eyes now, but I know she'll thank me later.

Remembering the big picture can also force a manager to practice tough love with his staff. You might have to make your people swallow bitter medicine for their own good. But it can be done without seeming cruel or cold. The Empathy Effect requires clear communication, and the empathetic manager lets his staff know that a little pain up-front will make their lives easier later on. The time when I had to sell my staff on the idea of the closing rehearsals was a perfect example. "Let's just give this a try. I really think it's going to save you time and stress in the long run."

## Learning to Listen

Of course, good communication isn't one-sided. The value of a leader's ability to clearly state his message to employees and customers drops by half if he's not also a good listener. To practice The Empathy Effect—and to participate in its benefits himself—the leader needs the listening skills to hear and understand his employees' concerns, as well as the sources of their pride. Otherwise, he won't know what to respond to.

Make no mistake about it—listening is a discipline. Some people might have more of a talent for it than others, but like any skill, listening requires practice and effort. It's easy to be a bad listener. Any slob can be one, and many of them are. But it takes hard work to learn how to listen to other people, to look them in the eye and listen patiently while they speak, to really try to understand what they mean and recognize the validity of their points of view. The bad listener impatiently darts his eyes around the room. With his sighs, jittery body language and pained expressions, he makes it clear that he doesn't want to hear what the other person has to say. He cuts people off and talks over them. Bad listeners make a choice to be bad listeners. It's a form of selfishness. They don't respect other people enough to make the effort to listen to them. In other words, bad listeners display a lack of empathy. But what goes around comes around: For the other person it's rude and insulting when the bad listener doesn't listen, but in the long run the bad listener only harms himself. Just as The Empathy Effect improves the situation for everyone involved, the lack of empathy displayed by bad listeners becomes a barrier. And barriers separate people. Not only will the bad listener and his employees stop understanding each other; they might stop knowing each other altogether. "Have a nice life."

## The Delicate Balance

Nonetheless, it's necessary to weigh the outcomes when demonstrating empathy. If you give too much, people might try to take advantage of you—whether they're your children, your employees, your customers or the world at large.

"Well, that was a nice guy who brushed against me in the New York subway. He said, 'Excuse me.'" Lo and behold, he picked your pocket.

Like listening, empathetic management requires the discipline to rein in your impulses—and not cross over, even when you know you can. Remember that scene in *An Officer and a Gentleman*, where Zack Mayo, the Navy Flight School recruit played by Richard Gere, wants to jump into the training pool to rescue his friend, who's trapped underwater in a cockpit-simulation cage? Hard-as-nails Gunnery Sgt. Emil Foley, played by Louis Gossett, Jr., forbids Mayo to interfere. He doesn't realize that the cage door is stuck and the trainee is about to drown. Invoking the discipline required of an empathetic leader, Foley stays focused on the long-term objective—which in this case is to prepare the young pilot for the real world of battle. Sgt. Foley knows that relieving the recruit's immediate discomfort would only harm him, maybe even kill him, in the long run. Despite loud protests from Mayo, Gunnery Sgt. Foley waits until the last possible second before he finally dives into the water and rescues the trapped man himself. When practicing The Empathy Effect as a leader, you have to make decisions about when to jump in, and when to hold back. When determining how much empathy to offer someone in a given situation, the business owner has to consider all three of his long-term goals—taking care of the customer, the profit and the employees.

## Setting a Reasonable Tone

In business, where your empathy lies depends on the unique selling propositions (USPs) that you offer. A discount retailer can't have too much empathy when someone complains about quality and service, and the premium-price company can't buckle when a customer asks for a discount. Is the customer really always right? Maybe only when they've agreed from the outset to the appropriateness of the price you're charging for the USPs that you promise to deliver.

Even so, a customer might occasionally become abusive to an employee. If some belligerent jerk starts bellowing obscenities and sexist remarks at my people, I can't be empathetic towards him. But what I came to realize was that by initiating The Empathy Effect with the customer in the first place, the business sets a tone of being reasonable—which, more often than not, the customer will recognize and reciprocate. When given a positive experience, customers who value empathetic products and services will probably not be jerky to your people. It's that circular, mutually beneficial nature of The Empathy Effect again. Empathy-based customers can see that you're doing the right thing, which is why they're willing to pay a reasonable premium in return. When the company is delivering an empathetic experience to the customers, only a real horse's ass would abuse the employees.

## Building an Empathetic Team

I thought a lot about team-building in an empathetic business culture. Many companies, including my own, succeed by having a core group of people as their leadership team. These senior managers are the mentors who pass along and sustain the company culture to the new hires. Without these leaders, the message of our mission and values wouldn't soak down through the layers of the company.

Having a core leadership team has only been possible because of the long tenures that our Empathy Effect culture has encouraged. The example starts with me (I hope), and flows down to Majestic Mortgage president Kevin McGovern, and then to Diane Schroeder, my executive VP of operations, and then to closings VP Carol Harper and her staff, etc. The customers benefit and, in turn, the company and the employees prosper.

Meanwhile, over on the dark side, there's bad old Mr. Clueless, whose antipathetic management style breeds so much resentment in his staff that they're constantly fleeing for the exits. There are no long tenures at his company, no senior people to carry on a positive company culture. Just as The Empathy Effect works in a self-perpetuating circle of mutual benefit, its opposite, the antipathetic environment, sucks out everything positive in a draining, downward spiral. The greedy, clueless business owner alienates his employees, whose short stints encourage him to disrespect his people and treat them as expendable resources, which in turn makes the employees bolt even faster. Customers get the same treatment, regarded as short-term, smash-and-grab opportunities. "Why not try to screw them?" Mr. Clueless figures. The negativity of this ego-driven atmosphere breeds like cancer cells.

## Every Member Plays a Role

In refreshing contrast, an Empathy Effect company culture is steered by a leader who not only respects the intelligence and hard work of his staff, but also recognizes and encourages their individual talents. Like any good manager of a professional sports team, the empathetic business owner realizes that each member of his staff has his or her own role to play. The organization's success is not dependent solely on one or two superstars, although the presence of such people definitely boosts the entire organization. Look at coach Phil Jackson, who led the legendary Chicago Bulls to six NBA championships during the team's heyday with Michael Jordan and Scottie Pippen in the 1990s. He knew that a team can't be composed solely of superstars, and that relying too much on any one player would tear the Bulls apart. A master at team-building, Jackson recognized the important contributions that each of his players made, as components of the whole. He managed all the egos to create the best team in basketball, demonstrating the leadership power of The Empathy Effect.

In any organization, the empathetic manager understands and can orchestrate the complex interrelationships among the efforts made by every person in the company, from the CEO to the receptionist and even the vendors. As always, an equitable profit-sharing program helps build an atmosphere of cooperation within the organization and between the departments.

When building a powerful and empathetic team, the leader's knack for recognizing and encouraging individual strengths not only serves the practical purpose of ensuring that all necessary functions are executed properly—it also fortifies each person's sense of their own purpose and worth. Most people have a particular specialty or talent to offer their organization, and who doesn't want to be appreciated and rewarded for the qualities that make them valuable? Whereas the antipathetic leader might deliberately try to squelch the potential he sees in his staff because it threatens him, a leader who embraces The Empathy Effect recognizes and nurtures each individual's pursuit of their highest human potential. He's not threatened because he knows that helping people be their best will only power the empathy wheel, and come back to benefit him, too.

With the employee's strengthened sense of value to the organization comes a higher level of professionalism, which promotes discipline and modesty. A mature, professional athlete knows when to step forward and when to hold back, even if it occasionally means spending a game on the bench. The pro recognizes how his skills fit into the overall team effort. He knows his role. You can see the same disciplined humility in professional musicians: The soloist might not play a single note for the first half of the song, waiting patiently for his cue to step into the spotlight. He makes his contribution based on what he knows the song requires, not on gratifying his ego.

## Building Faith among the Baton Passers

In any business, the salespeople are responsible for bringing in the transactions. Without them, there is no company. At the same time, without the backroom pumping out the orders for whatever product or service the company sells, the sales force will lose all credibility with the customers. Orders will either be delivered late, with poor quality, or not at all. In the mortgage business, loan originators need the assurance that when they bring in a new loan, the file will proceed flawlessly through the system.

But very often, the originator doesn't trust the backroom to meet the deadlines necessary to close the loan. The salesperson's reputation is at stake—and so is his income, since he's paid on commission. He might have multiple orders in the pipeline, or a million dollar account he has to entrust to the backroom. Without empathetic leadership to make sure the departments support and respect one another, the salesperson is reluctant to pass the baton, afraid to relinquish control. He tries to keep a finger or two on the baton as it moves through other hands in the process of the loan file being prepared. But his micromanagement causes more problems than it solves, bogging down the loan file's progress, while also insulting the operations people. In his reluctance to pass the baton, the salesperson shows that he doesn't have faith in the backroom. When the sales guy won't let go, the operations people never get the chance to prove their own trustworthiness. Worse, the salesman becomes incompetent by wandering out of his realm. The operations department is not his wheelhouse.

How do you run a relay race in business? How does an empathetic leader manage each of his team members' individual roles so that the people in the different departments can confidently pass the baton to each other, without wanting to constantly touch some part of it? The fact is, ideas for improving interdepartmental processes and strengthening trust between the employees lie at the levels of the people passing the batons. The mistake many companies make is that they don't give the rank-and-file a chance to suggest improvements. The dictatorial, antipathetic manager is not interested in the opinions of his people, and doesn't allow a voice for them. Conversely, the empathetic leader is strong and secure enough to create a forum for communication from the employees and between the departments. Maybe it's written or spoken, but through these communication channels conflicts are resolved and an atmosphere of greater trust and respect is cultivated.

Practicing The Empathy Effect means always thinking about what other people want—not necessarily because you're going to give it to them, but at least so that you will know the parameters in which you can deal with a particular person or department, the line that separates a home run from a foul ball. In a society like ours, where the complexity of modern life almost forces people to become self-involved, it takes discipline to set aside thoughts of our own needs and desires and to think instead about other people's motivations and points of view. Just as we ask, "What does the customer want?", and, "What does the employee want?", on a macro level we have to consider what each of the departments wants.

What's most important to the salesperson? His top priority is to make sure his customers are taken care of. That's why in many companies the salespeople are constantly trying to monitor the process of their customers' orders being filled as they wend through the company's various departments.

Come right out and ask the salesperson what she wants: "I want a free-flowing transaction with no hitches. I want an experience for my customers that's second to none."

In the typical, non-empathetic mortgage company, every salesperson wants to use the best processor in the shop. The bad processors don't inspire confidence that they'll get the job done right, and in a timely manner. Maybe that's because they lack empathy and have never bothered to understand the salesperson's point of view. The bad processor doesn't know what it's like to miss a contingency date or a closing, or to learn that funds are missing from the closing table. In a non-empathetic environment like this, the whole operation suffers.

Meanwhile, if you ask the operations department what they want, it's to keep the salespeople out of their hair. "If this guy would just quit bugging me, I could get the job done!"

Everyone in our company knows that if one department lets another down, we will all suffer the consequences. In the context of a mortgage business, if the processor dumps on the closer, the transaction gets screwed up. The processor has to have some empathy for the closer.

"Let's sit down together and understand this. Tell me what your frustrations are."

Leaders and team-builders who exercise The Empathy Effect are also more likely to look at a situation and say, "Show me why you're struggling with this task." The empathetic leader doesn't approach this inquiry in an accusatory or reproachful way. Maybe the problem doesn't lie with the employee at all, but with an inefficient process she has inherited.

"Holy cow, I didn't realize you had to go through 27 computer screens to finish this form. No wonder it's taking so long. We need to change this."

First the manager has enough empathy to recognize that the employee is having a problem, and then more important, she works with her to solve it.

## Empathetic Leaders Know Every Department

In a truly empathetic company culture, every department understands and appreciates the importance of every other department's contribution to achieving the entire organization's goals. One way I've cultivated that atmosphere of understanding in my own company has been by creating a leadership team of people who have each worked in several different departments over the years. They know what the people in the other departments are facing. Diane Schroeder, who heads our operations department, started as a processor and then became my assistant on the sales side. She saw deals coming in, took applications with customers, asked them for documentation upfront, etc. Today, if a salesperson tells her that he can't get the customer's documents at the beginning, she knows better.

Cross-trained leaders are also more empathetic to the employees' individual strengths and talents—and their particular needs and situations—and so they understand the importance of finding the right roles for people. Since the leaders themselves are multi-tasking, multi-talented byproducts of the company's various departments and disciplines, they don't have the counterproductive, hoarding mentality that less empathetic department managers display with their staffs. Matching people with the right departments and jobs has helped make our company successful. If an employee is working in the processing department but demonstrates sales talents, then we create the opportunity for that individual to see the benefits of coming to the sales side.

When a person has stood in your shoes before, even if it was years ago, they are more likely to feel empathy for you now. If Diane had never done the job of a processor, how would she know if what they're telling her is true, or that she's not asking them to do something that's unreasonable?

My wife Renee has a cleaning woman visit our house every Saturday afternoon for three hours. It's one of the luxuries that come with having a larger house. Still, Renee wants to raise our daughters right, so she makes them pick up their rooms before the cleaning woman arrives. Otherwise, she doesn't have to clean their rooms (including their bathrooms), and the girls have to do it themselves instead.

The young cleaning woman is from somewhere in Eastern Europe. "You always have nice things like this?" she asks Renee in her broken English, looking around at the furnishings in our house.

"Well, no," Renee replies. "I haven't."

"I think I knew that."

Renee treats the cleaning girl like a person, not a peon. My wife has empathy because earlier in her life, she was at a similar socio-economic level herself—working hard, but still with little money. The most empathetic leaders have walked before in their employees' shoes.

## Empathy Helps Identify and Solve Problems

People often inflict pain on others without even realizing it. But these unfortunate occurrences can be held to a minimum when we take the trouble to consider the other person's situation and point of view. In business, communication channels have to stay open to ensure smooth operations and minimal misunderstandings.

When something goes wrong with one of our loans, we conduct an "autopsy" of the loan file. If a particular loan caused a breakdown or bottleneck in the system, we examine its history to determine what caused the problem. That way, we can learn from the mistake and not repeat it. After an autopsy is performed, we usually find out that the loan file started off wrong. Maybe the originator didn't have the correct information at the beginning, but the flawed file went through the system anyway, like a virus waiting to sicken its host.

The loan autopsy is one way that we ease the flow of communication between our departments. You've got to find problems to solve them, and that requires communication. At the same time, the people whose mistakes might be uncovered by the loan autopsy need to be thick-skinned. Almost paradoxically, the ability to gracefully accept constructive criticism about ourselves is part of how we practice The Empathy Effect for others. Defensiveness is not empathetic, and if it obstructs possibilities for personal growth, then it's a limitation, not a way to protect ourselves. And the stronger a person's own esteem is, the more empathetic he will be towards other people. Of course, the more empathetically the critique is rendered, the more graciously the recipient is likely to accept it. In an empathetic working environment, employees know the owners or managers are not going to embarrass or demean them. Everybody in the organization needs to understand that management doesn't want to put them down, but rather to help them do a better job for the customers, the company and themselves. Otherwise, in our case at least, we would not be fulfilling our mission statement.

When striving to overcome systemic problems in your business, it's important to show progress: If your organization is screwing up 10 times out of 10, and then that rate drops to nine times out of 10 (and then to eight, seven, six, etc.), at least you know you're on the right track. Accountability and measurement devices are crucial. Look at FedEx, with its package-tracking system. An automatic e-mail lets you know that your package has left the warehouse and is on its way, and with your tracking number you can monitor its progress right up until it reaches your door.

We do something similar in our backroom, where reports show salespeople the progress of a loan file. "Just want to let you know, your appraisal has been ordered." We understand the importance of showing progress, because such communication inspires confidence.

## Learning to Fly

The confidence that an empathetic leader inspires should be like that of airplane passengers for the pilot. People flying aboard a commercial airliner don't usually question the pilot's actions. They trust him to get them where they're going safely. They know he's a professional with lots of experience. If the plane hits turbulence, the pilot will know what to do.

As a business owner you've got to be able to radiate that same level of confidence with your staff. Employees shouldn't question or challenge your every move, and you're more likely to earn their trust when you manage empathetically. The staff must have faith in the manager, so that the customer can have confidence in the staff.

Employees are more likely to lose confidence in a self-involved, non-empathetic leader, who has made it clear with his words and actions that he doesn't respect or appreciate his staff. When employees lose faith in the leader, they start second-guessing him—and that leads to the company's demise, through a mass exodus or a coup.

I don't mean to suggest that we never have problems at my company. As a business owner I've never been perfect. I've made plenty of mistakes, and sometimes I stray.

"My God, we forgot to listen to what the loan officers were saying!"

And we might lose one. But with The Empathy Effect as my guidebook, I know I'll never stray too far.

## Management by Walking Around

The idea of management by walking around is nothing new, but it remains an important part of empathetic leadership. In another illustration of the circular nature of The Empathy Effect, you have to be an empathetic leader in the first place to manage effectively by walking around. That way, the employees aren't afraid to see you coming. They're more willing to open up when you stop at their desk and ask sincerely, "How's everything going?" People are afraid when they think the boss is an egomaniac, that he's money hungry and has no empathy for them.

Besides gathering feedback from my department heads, I also get up and walk around myself. One time we discovered that we needed about 20% more capacity from the closing department. So we asked, "What's holding you back? Do we need to hire more people?" It turned out that the closers were wasting time because they had to stand in line to receive their documents from one printer that everyone shared. If the closers had individual printers at their workstations, they could increase their capacity by 20% without having to add staff. Within two hours, we went out and bought more printers.

Again I'm reminded of former Southwest Airlines CEO—and current chairman—Herb Kelleher, and his open-door policy for all levels of employees. The irony was that in the empathetic environment that Kelleher created, people were happy and probably walked into his office only rarely. The companies most in need of an open-door policy are the ones that, because of their antipathetic cultures, will probably always keep the executives' doors shut tight to the concerns of the rank-and-file.

The flip side of the confidence instilled by empathetic managers who walk around is that they're not afraid to ask employees for help during a downturn. As Jack Stack points out in his book *The Great Game of Business*, many employers are afraid to admit bad times to their employees. If you're leading a tightly knit group of people in a familial environment, you might be averse to showing them bad numbers. But the ironic reality is that the only people who can get you out of those bad numbers and bootstrap your company are the employees themselves. They're the ones on the front lines. They know what works and what doesn't. Even when external factors are pulling profitability down—rising interest rates, a recessionary economy—an empathetic company can always find ways to increase market share. Maybe it's through diversification of products or markets, or maybe you scale back on something, but when all hands are on deck, the company can grab a bigger share. And that's true no matter what your business is. But oftentimes as CEOs or entrepreneurial business owners, we try to fight the battle alone, because we're embarrassed about losing money. Don't let your pride stop you from empowering employees to suggest ways to survive a lean period. By asking for the employees' help, you gain their trust by demonstrating that you trust them yourself.

Deep down, employees want to help you through a lean cycle. And when their profit-sharing checks depend on the company weathering the storm, their motivation is not deeply buried, but bubbles just below the surface. They don't want to leave. People never relish the hassles and heartaches of finding a new job. They know it's stressful to go on interviews and start from scratch at a new company, learning and adjusting to a foreign culture. An empathetic manager realizes that his people don't want to leave, which is part of why he asks for their help. It's easy to see how greed and ego would blind an antipathetic leader to this simple truth.

## Invisible Empathy?

Sometimes as a leader practicing The Empathy Effect, you have to quietly pull strings behind the scenes to achieve an empathetic result for an employee or team member. Sheriff Andy Taylor on TV's *The Andy Griffith Show* was an empathetic leader. He would arrange things to create a better outcome for his Deputy Fife, without Barney even knowing it. But practicing The Empathy Effect in leadership doesn't mean carrying weak performers. Instead, it sometimes requires you to respond transparently to issues that you know your people are having, even your superstars. This one wants more authority, that one needs flexible work hours, the other is looking for experience in a different department, etc. The empathetic manager finds ways to improve the experience of his employees before they become dissatisfied. He envisions a solution before the problem has a chance to worsen. The employees might see only the end result, without realizing the trouble the leader has taken on their behalf.

## Empathetic Management Is Custom Management

The empathetic leader realizes that every human being has his or her own specific circumstances and point of view, and therefore a blanket, across-the-board management style won't work. Empathetic management is custom management. And customization is based on understanding the individual's particular needs and situation. In other words, it's based on empathy.

Recently I had to figure out a custom approach to manage a dilemma with someone on my staff. This individual was driving a 10-year-old car, which only became an issue for me when her job started requiring her to occasionally drive our out-of-town consulting customers between their hotel and our training center. Though she could probably have afforded a new car, this employee's father would not have approved of the expense. The amount of driving she had to do for the company was relatively small, but nonetheless important. Still, the situation didn't seem to warrant us buying a company car for her.

Fortunately, I found a solution that would satisfy everyone involved. For that particular year, I gave this employee slightly less in profit sharing than I otherwise might have, and instead agreed to pay a portion of her monthly payment for a new car. As far as her father was concerned, this was a company car—and to an extent, that was true. The decision to buy it was mine, not his daughter's. Now I don't have to worry about the appearance of her vehicle when she drives our clients, and the employee herself feels better as a human being, and enjoys her new car.

The key was that I had taken the time to listen and understand her situation. And although I had been planning my talk with her for a couple of days, I made it appear spontaneous one afternoon as we passed each other in the office hallway.

"Hey, how's it going? By the way, we haven't talked about this yet, but I was wondering...."

If I had scheduled the meeting and given her time to think about it, she might not have been so candid with me. Of course, I had to maintain a delicate balance, asking myself, "Is the situation with her father really my business, and should I even get involved?" An empathetic leader knows when to jump in and when to hold back. I had to consider how my decision would affect other people, not just the advantage it would give me.

Chapter Seven

# *The Empathy Effect on Negotiating*

ost of the principles that I now recognize as key to The Empathy Effect first occurred to me as unconscious impulses. A sort of instinctive empathy had propped up my values ever since my days of tossing Mrs. Wantuck's newspaper onto her front stoop, but it wasn't until decades later that I realized empathy was the single biggest force to make or break a business deal. If either of the parties involved comes away embittered, then the negotiation was not empathetic and it won't lead to future deals. Both sides have to understand each other's points of view.

## Brother, Can You Swap 50 Cents for a Dollar?

It's the mid-1980s, and I'm with a group of real estate agents on a junket to Atlantic City. The trip has no pretense whatsoever of being about business—it's strictly for fun, and everybody knows that. It's going to be a very long day of fun, however, starting early in the morning aboard a charter plane, on the first flight out from Chicago. We're scheduled to fly back at 11 o'clock that night.

We land well before lunch and are whisked from the tiny Atlantic City airport straight to the casinos, for a whirlwind day of gambling and goofing off. The day is constant action. We're trying to fit in everything we can, seeing all the different casinos and trying slots, blackjack, craps—every variety of gambling they had. Everyone is having a good time.

At the end of this marathon day, we're completely exhausted as they shuttle us back to the airport. We've had a few cocktails. We're tapped out.

When we arrive at the airport, it hits me: It's almost 11 o'clock at night, and we've forgotten to eat. At the time, the Atlantic City airport is tiny and there's almost nothing in it. There are no restaurants, and the handful of concession stands are all closed for the night. We're starving, sitting there waiting for a two-hour flight, during which no meals will be served.

And then I spot a vending machine. It's amazing, but there are actually some of those rubber sandwiches inside. The machine is refrigerated, so I'm not worried about the food being spoiled.

But the problem is that we've just been through the casinos, and we have no change. None. When you're an amateur gambler finishing a day like this, whether it's in Atlantic City or Las Vegas, you've put your last quarter into a slot machine and yanked the lever.

So we're at this rinky-dink airport, it's 11 o'clock at night, the vending machine is the only place to eat, it doesn't accept bills, and we have no change. When I go to use the bill changer, I find that it doesn't work. We can see the food in the vending machine, but we can't buy it.

About 200 passengers have arrived at the airport and are waiting to board the plane. I'm really hungry and so are my wife and our friends, so I start walking around the terminal.

"Excuse me, do you have change for a dollar?"

Maybe the other people have already eaten, and they're not hungry. But nobody has the correct change. They've all been in the same situation as we have, throwing their coins into the slot machines. But I persist.

"Excuse me, do you have change for a dollar?"

"Let me check. Nope, sorry. I've only got 60 cents."

I keep walking around, asking all the people I can find.

"Sorry, I've only got 80 cents."

"Let's see. Twenty-five, 30, nope, only 40 cents."

I'm starting to feel frustrated. I can't make the deal, because no one's got change for a dollar. But I also feel the wheels turning—somewhere inside of me, I'm enjoying the challenge of finding a creative solution to this dilemma. My hunger pains are so bad that I find myself asking, *What's a dollar really worth in this situation?* It's worth whatever amount of change somebody is willing to give me for it.

So I decide that I'm willing to take 80 cents on a dollar, 65 cents, even 45 cents. People probably think I've got some trick up my sleeve, but they can't resist trading their coins for my dollar bills.

After a while I've got a pocketful of change. By the time I finish working the terminal, I've accumulated five or six dollars worth of coins, even though I've spent about $10 to get them.

Luckily I had singles to trade for the coins. But what if I'd only had fives, or tens—or twenties? Would I have traded larger bills for less than a dollar's worth of change? It would all depend on how badly I wanted those rubber sandwiches.

## Let's Make an Empathetic Deal

Anything that I could have found to eat would have been better than going hungry. So I said to myself, "This deal makes sense." It would let me take care of myself, my family and my friends.

"Does anybody want anything?"

They all looked at me in amazement. "Wow, you got some change. How in the world did you do that?!"

It was a win-win. The people trading their change for my dollar bills might have thought I was crazy, but they clearly came away with a profit.

The experience reminded me that whenever I negotiate anything, I've got to have empathy for the people on the other end to make the deal work. When the terms of a deal are based on both parties understanding and accommodating each other's needs and situations, the deal is more likely to be a success. The deal will feel right when there's mutual empathy on both sides, when The Empathy Effect works its magic.

My Atlantic City rubber-sandwich deal also taught me that the value of anything gained through negotiation is subjective—varying with the tastes and circumstances of the people involved. To successfully negotiate deals, I had to understand what was important to the other party, and to make an offer that respected the priorities of both sides.

## My First Big Deal

When I was negotiating to buy my first Century 21 real estate office from a former employer in 1982, I didn't know the whole story behind his business. I had been working as a real estate agent in this man's Antioch, Illinois, location for a few years when one day he asked me, "Hey Tom, want to buy my Mundelein office? I'll give you a sweetheart deal."

As it happened, I had been seriously considering becoming my own boss anyway. I suppose he knew that, and his offer seemed fair: I would pay $10,000 for the franchise, $4,000 down and $6,000 over time. Maybe he was having some empathy for me, thinking, "Here's a guy who's worked for me for a while, he's done some great things for me, and now he's willing to buy my business. I'll give him a terrific price."

As I heard later, there were reasons why this man was eager to unload the office at a sharp discount, with easy financing terms. A few years before, shortly after he had bought the office himself, the man received an announcement from the regional office of the company. They were bringing in some big-shooter salesman from another real estate franchise to open an office not far from his, in the same town. And since the company had a "quarter of a mile" rule that required its franchises to be at least that far apart, the guy who was there first would have to go. This must have been a severe kick below the belt for him, since his own business had been limping along and the region wanted to bring in a powerhouse to shove him out of the way. Feeling betrayed, he sued. He argued that the two offices might have been within a quarter mile as the crow flies, but they were farther apart for people driving. He lost his case but appealed, and eventually the region gave him a settlement that was probably more than what I ended up paying for his franchise.

Nonetheless, the deal was a good match for both of us. We would both benefit from it. After working as an employee for years, I was now buying my own business. For his part, the seller could afford to let the franchise go for a reduced price, thanks to the settlement he'd received from the region. And maybe more important, he didn't want to be in that town anymore, in the shadow of the big shooter who had just come blazing onto the scene. By selling when he did, my former boss managed to avoid an ugly situation. I felt confident that there was still plenty of business to go around, and I wasn't worried about the new hotshot in town.

Empathy seemed present in this win-win scenario, even though I didn't learn the background of the situation until after the deal was done. Luckily for me, I wasn't hurt by not knowing all the circumstances upfront. I had taken a huge step in acquiring my first business. Things were starting to happen. I still had a big following of customers in the Lake Villa area, and wound up buying a second real estate office there. I knew I should have a presence in that market. I started small and later developed a shopping center next to a McDonald's, and moved the office there.

## Understanding the Other Guy

My first experience with truly empathetic negotiation would come a few years later, in 1988, when I bought my third real estate office, in the more upscale Chicago suburb of Libertyville. The experience reminded me that the value of anything negotiated lies in the eyes of the beholder. The seller and I both had specific goals: I wanted to buy an existing Century 21 franchise in the North Shore market of Libertyville, and he was ready to sell. It was only a question of how we could come together on the price. The problem was that he believed his business was worth $10,000 more than I did.

"I think $30,000 is a fair price," he said.

"But I think it's only worth $20,000," I told him.

We had reached a crucial point in the negotiations, where the deal might have hit the skids if we let ego take over. Ego kills The Empathy Effect, and it poisons any attempt at empathetic negotiations. That's why so many deals go bad.

For the moment at least, there seemed to be a $10,000 impasse between our respective assessments of what his business was worth. But I wanted to have some empathy for his point of view. I had to come over to his side, to see the deal with his vision, through his filter. I had to find out what was really on his mind.

"I'm just curious," I said. "But tell me: Why do you think this franchise is worth $30,000?"

"Here's what's happened," he said. "I just hired two new salespeople, and I really believe they're going to be superstars during the next year. If I were to wait 12 months to sell my business, I honestly think I could get 30 grand for it, based on the production of these two new people."

It was as simple as asking him a question. Now I knew where he was coming from, and I could try to structure a win-win deal. Once I had his information, and my own, I looked for a creative way to put it all together. People might look at a particular negotiation and say, "Well, that's never been done before." It doesn't matter, as long as the solution works.

The seller thought one of the new agents would become a multi-million-dollar producer over the coming year—which by itself would generate more revenue for the company. If his prediction came true, I was willing to give him a taste of that upside. After all, he would have created it by hiring the superstars.

I could have tried to take advantage of him: "You're all wet. These guys aren't as good as you say they are."

But that's not me, and such an attitude would have sunk the deal. So I asked him, "Could we structure this so that I pay you what I think the business is worth, but I give you all the upside if these two salespeople do what you say they're going to do?"

If after 12 months they had reached the plateau he was promising, I would give him the extra $10,000. He would get what he believed his business was worth.

"We can settle the date right now," I told him. "You'll come back to see me, and if these two people have lived up to your expectations, I will write you a check for $10,000. I'll give you full authority to obtain production reports from the regional office for those two employees, so you can conduct your own audit."

It was an empathetic offer that he couldn't refuse. "Tom, you've got yourself a deal."

Empathy made sure the deal would be fair for both of us. And it was a good thing, too. After 12 months, the "superstar" salesmen did not live up to the hype. My expectations were much lower than the seller's, but these two barely made the numbers I had hoped for. At the end of the 12 months, the seller came back to me, ready to claim his 10 grand bonus. And then he read the production reports. "Boy, I really thought they'd do better...."

In an ego-driven negotiation, the buyer becomes stubborn and angry: "There's no way this thing is really worth what he's asking." It's easy to see how that lack of empathy would slam the brakes on the deal. Without empathy, the parties negotiating don't take the trouble to get into each other's heads and find out what's important to both sides. They don't know what the deal is really worth to each party, so it falls dead in the water. And even if the deal manages to come off, without empathy it's going to be either a win-lose or a lose-win. Somebody will get burned.

When I was negotiating to buy my Libertyville office, The Empathy Effect not only made the transaction possible, but it also ensured that we would survive the deal. Both parties would still respect one another, with no bitter feelings. The Empathy Effect provided the structure. If I had paid the entire $30,000 he asked for, I would have later become upset and regretted the deal. I probably would have blamed the other guy: "He overcharged me." On the other hand, the seller would have been left feeling bitter if I had put the squeeze on him: "You're going to take $20,000 for this franchise, because the whole thing is going down the toilet anyway. I'm doing you a favor."

I'm sure he was disappointed that he didn't get his $10,000 bonus, but he probably also realized how fortunate he had been for selling the business when he did. If he had waited a year, and watched his dreams of superstar production evaporate, he wouldn't have gotten even $20,000 for it. He might have even gone out of business. Luckily for me, I had my own superstar staff. The business did well under my leadership. The seller, on the other hand, had dodged a bullet by selling his franchise at the right time. And he didn't have to feel bad about his conduct in the negotiations, because he hadn't ripped me off.

The deal worked seamlessly for me. I paid a one-time cost of $20,000 to acquire a branded, Century 21 franchise in the market I wanted to enter, and I did not have to pay a penny more at the end of the 12 months. Negotiating with The Empathy Effect also means remembering empathy for your own position. You have to protect your own rights as you craft an attractive offer for the other party. I wasn't dumb enough to give the seller $30,000 and then have to chase him for a ten-grand refund a year later. That would have meant letting myself down. For me this deal was no-harm, no-foul. I felt comfortable paying $20,000, and would have happily handed over 10 grand more if the seller's staff had met their targets. In that case the business would have been worth the $30,000 he had wanted. I could tell that he genuinely believed these people would be superstars. He was not bluffing. He was totally earnest. I could feel it in my gut.

People have asked me how I learned to structure deals like this, since I never had much formal business training. Looking back, it's clear that I was following my instincts, which were rooted in the empathy and responsibility that my parents had instilled in me as a kid. Trusting my instincts helped me find a creative solution to the $10,000 impasse. I had to be resourceful to survive.

## The Empathy Effect and Good Reputation

I learned that the most resourceful approach, and the best way to strike an agreement when negotiating with another person, was to feel empathy for them. Just as I had worried about my obligation to deliver Mrs. Wantuck's newspaper, I was concerned about the other person when I negotiated to buy my Libertyville office. Otherwise, the deal—and my reputation—would not have stood the test of time. Reputation is huge in the business world. This was a fair deal, and that's something people remember. A fair deal especially sticks out in someone's mind when they've been cheated or disrespected in other negotiations.

I've had employees turn down lucrative job offers from headhunters because, as they've told me, they respected my values and honesty. And they weren't so sure about the values and honesty of the other guy. Being rewarded for your good reputation is a perfect example of The Empathy Effect, a self-perpetuating circle that benefits everyone involved. Positive input creates more of the same for years to come, even across generations. A person's reputation becomes his human resumé, the sum history of his attitudes and actions, the way he treats others and the reliability and quality of his work and character.

When The Empathy Effect shines through a business negotiation, the people involved are far more likely to survive the deal, to come away from it feeling good about what they've accomplished. Surviving the deal means there are no ill feelings between the parties. Everyone involved knows that they were treated fairly and they gained something worthwhile from the transaction. Mutual respect is built on both sides. The Empathy Effect works its magic.

## Relationships, or Just Transactions?

A company's reputation often hinges on whether it offers its customers relationships, or just transactions. Transactional companies are ego-driven: Grab the money, and don't worry about burning bridges. But a company's bad reputation can build fast, and last a very long time in people's memories.

A relationship-based company, on the other hand, forms bonds and loyalty by taking care of its customers—and its employees, vendors and suppliers, etc. Customers learn quickly which type of company they're dealing with. Small gestures and attention to detail go a long way. People pick up on the empathetic signs that help create loyal customers—like the online shopping cart, checkout and receipt from the Macy's website, each of which include a little photograph and description of every item you buy online, to help you remember what you've selected; or the car wash you pay for at the gas pump, with a receipt code that's good for 30 days in case you would rather come back later; or the placard in the mortgage company lobby that's personalized to greet customers arriving for their appointments. On the other hand, consumers also quickly see the signs when the business has no empathy for them and only wants the transaction—the convenience store cashier who still doesn't say hello or know your name after four years, the guy in the smoothie shop who sighs with annoyance when a customer approaches the counter, the surly video store clerk who slams down your change and refuses to make eye contact, the big-box retailer that tries to pick your bones clean before you can walk out the door with that new DVD player. Unless there's some counterbalancing show of empathy, or a blatant platform of lowest price, the transactional company will only hold on until something better comes along for the consumer. Then it's, "See you later, Charlie."

Customers aren't the only ones who know the difference between transaction and relationship companies; the employees feel it most of all. It's easy to tell if your boss is a stand-up guy who will go to the wall for you, or if he's an egoist who will dump you the minute his business takes even the slightest downturn.

Relationship companies have better reputations, and a good reputation is The Empathy Effect come full circle. When people reward you with their loyalty and affection because you've been good to them in the past—keeping your word, delivering quality work and a great experience, paying your bills promptly—you can almost see the empathy wheel turning. The best reputations stand the test of time, as The Empathy Effect builds a safety net around you, your family and your business.

## What's a Contract Really Worth?

When your good reputation reflects The Empathy Effect back onto you and your business, it also changes the nature of written contracts. Years ago, people did business on a handshake. Their word was enough.

"I know him. I know his parents. I've done business with him before. He's got a great reputation."

Today, many businesspeople try to put themselves in the forefront of the deal by insisting on a written contract. But what good does a contract really do? It's there for the letter of the law, but would the parties in the deal actually sue each other? Why would things come to that point in the first place? Lawsuits are probably more common for huge corporations dealing with multimillion-dollar deals, but are small businessmen and entrepreneurs really going to sue their clients or vendors? Or their former employees?

When The Empathy Effect has been practiced in the negotiations and in the execution of the deal, the contract becomes less of a legal protection than a letter of understanding between the parties. "What was our deal, again?"

When the time came for me to sell my Mundelein Century 21 office, The Empathy Effect made the deal. We had a contract, but not much of a need for it. I sold the franchise to someone I knew very well, a woman who had been working for me in that very office. Right from the beginning, I could see that this deal would be a win-win. I had been wanting to sell the office for a while. After I bought another franchise in the more affluent suburb of Libertyville, I soon found that I could service my clients in Mundelein from the new office, but not the other way around. A trustworthy buyer would be a godsend for me. I asked myself, "Who's the most likely buyer for this office? Probably somebody who's already inside of it."

This woman had been managing the office as my employee, and had mentioned that she would like to run her own business someday. So I offered to sell her the franchise. She wanted to take a shot at it. The problem was that she didn't have a lot of cash. So I decided to let her buy the business for little money down. I would provide the balance and she would pay me in monthly installments. It was a true win-win: She would acquire her own business with little money down, and I would be free to devote my full attention to my Libertyville and Lindenhurst locations, plus the mortgage company I had just started. The Mundelein office had become an albatross for me, and now I wouldn't have to worry about it anymore.

I felt good knowing that I had left the business in a good state for her. I didn't steal any of her people; the same staff remained in place after she bought the franchise. I felt an obligation to make the whole thing work for her. My mortgage company was located in the same strip center, so I was close by and could mentor her during the transition.

The deal gave us both clear benefits. But as always, their value was in the eyes—and the circumstances—of the beholders. The office I was selling had become incompatible with my new business strategy, but it could still be a prosperous enterprise for the right owner who wanted to concentrate in the local market. This woman lived and worked in Mundelein. She knew the area and could serve the market well. Acquiring the franchise for little money down was like a windfall from above for her, but the arrangement also benefited me, too. And it wasn't as risky as it might have seemed: I was in a partnership that owned the building where she leased the office, so I was one of her landlords. I sold her the business for a little below scale. I had a rent reprieve for a short period, and let the lease go to market when I sold her the business.

The best deals are the ones that you can tell were meant to be. They feel right. It's almost as if The Empathy Effect creates the opportunity for the deal to exist in the first place, before you even reach the point of negotiating its terms. For me in this case, The Empathy Effect started by looking at her situation and understanding it, which gave me the idea to sell her the franchise. But I also had to determine what I wanted for myself—what was my vision for the future of my business? What did I want it to look like? Could I really service Libertyville from Mundelein, and did I even want to be in that market, even though it was the first office I had bought and it held some sentimental value for me? The answers pointed straight to the deal we made.

Through the monthly installments, she paid me everything she owed. But running the business profitably turned out to be more difficult than it appeared. I consider myself the perfect, 17-year, overnight success. From the outside, it always seems easy. On the inside, people find out, "Holy smokes! It's hard to make money!" A couple of years later, she moved on and merged with another company.

## If Your Heart's Not in It, the Deal's Not Right

When the day came to sell my remaining Century 21 offices, the experience was bittersweet for me. A couple of homebuilders I had done business with approached me about buying my Libertyville and Lindenhurst offices, which at the time represented my entire real estate company. But I really didn't want to sell. I wasn't interested—and I told them so, repeatedly.

"It's not for sale. But thanks for asking."

Despite my flat refusals, one of the builders in particular kept pushing me to sell. He must have asked me 20 times. He and his partner were itching to buy my company and enter the residential brokerage business. Maybe it seemed simple to them.

Finally, after the umpteenth time that he asked me to reconsider, I reluctantly agreed to a meeting. This builder had denoted the land and constructed a huge church on an intersection in Lake Forest, one of Chicago's wealthiest, old-money suburbs. The meeting would take place down the road from the church, in the palatial home he had built for his family.

Back then I barely had two nickels to rub together. I thought I had to put on a suit and tie just to visit Lake Forest. But there I was, sitting upstairs in the den of this beautiful house, talking with the two partners who wanted to buy my business.

"All right," I said. "Let's talk some numbers here."

I could negotiate from a position of power only because I saw

how badly these two wanted the deal. At the time I had more than 50
agents working for me, and the builders thought they could take the
business to a higher level.

Finally, even though it didn't feel quite right to me, I gave in and
agreed to sell. The number ended up being about $140,000. But since
I wasn't really interested in selling, I decided that if I were going to
leave the business, it would have to be completely on my terms.

"It's a good number," I said. "But it has to be all cash. I won't accept any financing terms."

My wife Renee was still managing one of the offices, along with
Jan Kosatka, who'd been with us a long time and owned a small amount
of stock in one of the companies.

"You also have to take care of these two ladies," I told them. "No
desk fees for two years."

"Okay," the man said. "Sign the deal."

## The Empathy Wasn't There

Looking back on it, I realize that selling my real estate business was
not an empathetic deal. My heart wasn't in it. The builders knew what
they wanted for themselves, but the deal was one-sided, without any
mutual empathy. All the zeal for the deal was coming from the buyers.
Maybe that's why the experience left a bitter aftertaste for me. When
I sold my Century 21 franchises I also left behind lots of employees
and colleagues in real estate, many of whom I had given their starts
in the business.

Selling was hard enough, but it got worse later when I watched
the new owners take the company down the drain. They foolishly
abandoned the franchise name, letting ego take over and re-branding the business with one of the new executive's names instead. So it
didn't really surprise me to learn that one of the owners was also an
arrogant and antipathetic manager, who quickly alienated the staff
with his "my way or the highway" approach. Instead of just plugging
into the franchise system, it was as if he had bought a McDonald's
and decided to start selling hotdogs. Renee continued to work there

and service her clients, but she ended up leaving a year later. Eventually the whole operation sank under the waves. The new owner had torpedoed his business with a lack of empathy.

The deal never felt right in my gut, and to an extent I failed myself with this lack of self empathy. Of course, it wasn't all bad: Profit from the sale was a boon for my family and my mortgage company. But unlike when I sold my Mundelein office to a former employee for little money down, this time I didn't have any future interest in the business, nor did I particularly care about the two guys who had bought the offices for cash. The more important factor was my reputation. Luckily for me, the new owner changed the name of the business immediately after buying it, so that by the time the company crumbled, any association it had with my name had long since passed. My reputation wasn't tarnished by the sale. In retrospect I also realize that it was because I had sold my real estate business that I was able to make my mark in the mortgage industry—another plus. And as it turned out, I could do more for the real estate community by creating a mortgage company with empathy-based USPs than I could by working in the real estate business itself.

## Empathy for Business Partners

Sometimes strengthening a deal through empathy also depends on how well you choose and understand your partners. I learned this lesson during the early 1980s, when I joined forces with my brother-in-law, Mark De Rue, and our friend Jeff Krol, to buy three small apartment buildings in the far-flung Chicago suburb of Round Lake Beach. The apartment complex had four buildings, each with four units. Three of the four buildings had gone into foreclosure and been taken back by the lender, the State Bank of Little Rock, Arkansas. This was during the days of the savings-and-loan crisis in America, and the bad debt of these three buildings was dragging on the books of this little institution.

We weren't looking to invest in apartment properties, but then the deal presented itself when Mark spotted it. Most of the 12 units

were leased, so there would be monthly rental income from the investment. The asking price seemed unbelievably low—less than $200,000
for the three buildings, or about $15,000 per unit. Of course, when
something looks too good to be true, it probably is. People rightly
back away from deals for that reason. But since this was during the
S&L crisis, when many small lending institutions were sagging under
the burden of bad debt, I was willing to look closer at the deal and
see whether it made any sense.

So we started looking into it. We said, "Let's do our homework.
Let's investigate why this building hasn't sold, and why it's priced so
low." The buildings had brick construction, and were not in bad shape.

I decided we had to travel to Little Rock and negotiate face-to-
face with the people at the S&L. Mark and I made arrangements to
fly down on the 3rd of July. Jeff didn't come with us, but I remember
signing the offer on the hood of his car at a softball game, before
heading to the airport. The next available flight back to Chicago was
on the 5th, so Mark and I would end up spending the 4th of July in
Little Rock, away from our families. When we got there, most of the
businesses in town were closed for the holiday. The fireworks display
was not what we were used to back home. Just to order cocktails, we
had to buy private memberships at a local club.

At the S&L we presented our offer. We would acquire the
three, four-unit apartment buildings for $240,000, with 20 grand
down. They jumped at it. They were glad to get the properties off
their books.

But when it came time to wire the financing, we ran into a hitch
that explained why the properties had been priced so low. No one
wanted to finance the deal. It turned out that the buildings had
become dead weight for the lender for good reason: The units were
leased to renters, but they were classified as having condominium
ownership. One investor had owned all of the condo units before they
slid into foreclosure. It's hard to believe now with America's ongoing
condo craze, but during the early 1980s, properties with condominium
ownership suffered from a terrible public image. People thought that
once you bought one, you couldn't get rid of it. Especially during the

days of the S&L scandal, no lender would finance the purchase of condominium properties. The risk was too high.

We figured out that the deal could be worth lots of money—if only it were finance-able. We pulled the Covenants, Conditions and Restrictions of Record, and the condominium documents. We found that if we could get the buildings out of condominium status, and revert them to being rental apartments, we would qualify for FHA financing. With help from an attorney that Jeff knew downtown, we took the necessary legal steps and dissolved the condominium association. Each building became a four-unit property, and with Jeff's connections and personal net worth, we got the financing and acquired them. With the condo stigma now gone, their value immediately shot up by almost 150%. Even better, since the FHA loan could be assumed by a new buyer, the properties would be easier to sell. We refinanced the loan to recover our equity, and eventually wound up selling the buildings for a total of $450,000, after paying just $240,000 for them only a few years earlier. An outside buyer acquired two, and with a minimal down payment Mark bought the third building, at a reduced price. He still owns it today.

Even the owner of the fourth building benefited from the spreading ripples of The Empathy Effect. By removing the condo label, we had made it possible for him to sell, since a buyer could now secure financing. And the seller would make a big profit.

When we did the deal in 1985, times were tough. People were saying the sky was going to fall: "Why would you want to buy three apartment buildings in Round Lake Beach?" Mortgage rates were high, but the rental market was lagging behind the stronger demand that would be created if more people put off buying homes. Monthly rent for a one-bedroom apartment was only about $450. If you had to pay condominium rates for financing, the deal would not cashflow. As it turned out, condominium ownership was before its time. Today, the bad press has faded from people's memories, and everyone thinks condos are the greatest thing in the world.

This deal would not have worked without The Empathy Effect that occurred when Jeff and I formed the partnership to buy the properties, and we agreed to let Mark help out in exchange for the chance to participate in the future upside. The structure of the partnership was critical. Jeff was the vehicle to get the financing, and he knew the lawyers downtown. I was the dealmaker with experience in the real estate business. Mark found the property. He was young and going through law school. He poured sweat-equity in the deal, cleaning and repairing the buildings, collecting rent from the tenants. There were a few vacant units that he had to lease up, some broken windows and carpeting that needed to be replaced. We practiced The Empathy Effect for the partnership by honestly assessing our individual talents: Who was best at what? "What is it that you want to do, and what is it that you don't want to do?" That's how we built the partnership, and it worked. We made a lot of money on the deal by playing to each other's strengths. It was a truly empathetic business venture—we understood our team, the seller's predicament and the situation with the properties.

Without financing, the seller would have needed a cash buyer. But what cash buyer would want to have to clean up the mess in those buildings? Before we came along, the problem with the properties, besides the lack of financing, was that the seller had not found the right match between a buyer and the buildings. A successful, empathetic deal needs an essence match, just like with hiring employees or forming a business partnership. A cash buyer probably would have been a white-collar guy who wouldn't want to do all the dirty work required to make the deal pay off. Someone like that looking for an investment opportunity probably was not going to do this deal. The waters would be too unfamiliar to him. He wouldn't understand the condominium side. Our partnership managed to cover all of the bases, and we did very well in the deal.

## Empathy Finds Solutions

Back in the late 1970s when I was selling homes as prime soared to 17%, I learned to look for creative, empathetic ways to make deals work. With rates higher than Everest, it was almost a miracle that we managed to do a deal a day for 180 straight days, with my staff of 10 real estate agents, in a town of only 5,700 people. We did it by having total empathy for the borrower and the circumstances of the national economy at the time.

In the early years of Fannie Mae, a clause in its documents indicated whether the mortgage qualified for a resale program. If so, the loan and its terms could be assumed by the next owner of the property. Assumable mortgages from past years had much lower interest rates, giving both the buyer and the seller big advantages. People who had taken out mortgages a few years earlier at 13% might never have dreamed that someday someone would want to assume a loan with such a high nut. But when rates shot up to 17%, and even to 21%, by comparison the old loans at 13% began to seem like bargains. At the time, people were making their home-buying decisions based solely on monthly payment, and at the lower rate, these homes became affordable. Just as years later my partners and I would dig into the mystery of why the apartment buildings in Round Lake Beach hadn't sold, back then we took a closer look at what might have seemed like an impossible situation. And lo and behold, we found an empathetic solution that knocked one over the bleachers for our client's negotiating power. We just had to find houses with Fannie Mae resale clauses in their mortgages, and then convince the sellers to list their homes with us. Most of the time, people didn't even realize it when their mortgages were assumable. It wasn't something that was ever published or widely known.

"Listen, you might be thinking about selling your house, or maybe not," we would say. "But don't think about not selling because you believe the times are bad. If you really want to sell your house, we might be able to find a buyer, because you've got a Fannie Mae resale clause on your mortgage."

We began making deals, and the momentum started rolling. We would take 12% assumable mortgages and blend them with new money at 21%, to get a hybrid rate of 13.5%. People were saying, "Wow, this is the greatest thing in the world!" And they would end up buying a house that they previously thought they could never afford.

As a real estate agent representing buyers and sellers, I had to look at both sides with total empathy. In that context I was almost more of an arbitrator than a negotiator. By finding a creative way to put a home on the market with a lower mortgage-interest rate than otherwise comparable properties could offer, we benefited the seller, the buyer, and ourselves—an Empathy Effect grand slam!

Nevertheless, when showing homes to potential buyers, I would often run into the same stumbling block: People had the misconception, planted in their heads by some well-meaning parent or uncle, that they must always negotiate 8% off the sales price, no matter what. If the house was listed for $100,000, they would offer $92,000. And then the seller would get ticked off, and the deal would fall apart.

But here's what was really happening: People would go out and look at 10 houses, all in the same general price range. The one they wanted to buy was well worth a price in the upper 90s, probably even close to $100,000. But they would get hung up thinking they had to shave 8% off the asking price. I looked for a solution that wouldn't alienate the buyer.

"You've gone out and looked at ten houses, and you believe this one is the best. The only thing holding you back is that you think you have to negotiate eight percent off the asking price. The sellers have just reduced the price to $100,000 from $110,000, and they really need to get out of the house for their own personal reasons. Before we write this situation off as hopeless, let's just do this: Give me an hour to go back and talk to the sellers. I'm going to ask them to put the house back on the market at the original price of $110,000. Then you can make an offer for $100,000, and that way you'll feel better and still do the deal, right?"

People would look at me dumbfounded. "But that would be kind of stupid, wouldn't it?"

"Well, yeah. It really would be. So why don't you just offer $100,000 right now? You're still going to wind up in the same place. And it's a fair price."

Lo and behold, we'd make the deal.

## Letting Go of Ego

In the summer of 2004, I joined some partners to buy an office building that will be the new headquarters of Majestic Mortgage Corporation and Majestic Consulting & Marketing, Inc. Buying the building turned out to be a great deal, but I very nearly let my ego kill the negotiations.

The 28,000-square-foot, low-rise building is located in a professional office park in Vernon Hills, Illinois, a northern suburb of Chicago. Besides giving us more space and an upgraded office environment, the building also has other tenants to provide rental income from the investment. We had clearly outgrown our old space, a maze of offices and corridors cobbled together in five phases during years of incremental expansions. In the beginning we couldn't afford a bigger place, so as the company grew we just added on—and added on, and added on. The office space didn't flow properly. But we had never thought we would grow this big, and now it was time to move on. Still, I wasn't really in the market to buy a new building. That was until one day, when a commercial real estate agent named Dan Bessey brought the property to my attention. At the time, the building wasn't even for sale, but he could see that it would be perfect for us.

"I think this is a good opportunity, Tom. You should take a look at it."

So I did, and he was right. Not only would the building provide a more comfortable space for my growing staff, but it would also give us a more professional image in the national marketplace. There's a good hotel across the street, which is ideal because I'm now conducting my seminars in-house. Our guests will only have to walk across the parking lot. (The Empathy Effect was starting already.) The new office would be closer to the expressway, making it more convenient for our customers and some of our employees. Dan is a great commercial real estate agent. He showed great empathy by spotting the building in the first place, and by having the vision to recognize how well it would suit our particular needs. The fact that he understood our situation so well demonstrated tremendous empathy on his part. As The

Empathy Effect would have it, Dan would even wind up becoming a partner in the deal.

His insight helped bring the transaction to market. Before long, the owners were willing to sell, and I was making them an offer. At one point, I had the deal wired for around $2.4 million. And then, at the 11th hour, another bidder suddenly appeared, waving some ridiculous number, like $2.45 million.

At first I became emotional. "Well, screw that. I'm not going to buy this thing."

My ego got involved. My feelings were hurt. "I can't believe you did this to me." I let all these bad distractions creep into my thinking. "Our interest in the property created this deal," I grumbled to myself. "It wouldn't exist without us. The building wasn't even for sale. There was no price. We brought the deal to market and got them to set a price." I felt betrayed that the seller would disrespect our initial agreement and entertain a slightly higher offer from a newcomer. I was ticked off. "They just took a hundred grand out of my pocket!"

After a while I calmed down and began to consider the deal in more practical terms. I had invested lots of time into it. I had partners that I wanted to take care of. And despite the last-minute surprise, *the deal still felt right.*

I took a deep breath and told myself, "Forget about everything that's happened in the past. If this building came on the market right now, at $2.5 million, would the numbers still make sense? The answer is yes. Does the deal cash-flow at the extra hundred grand? Of course. Does it make sense, is it the right thing to do? Absolutely."

On the other hand, did I have a back-up plan? That answer was no. If the whole thing had fallen through, I wouldn't have known what to do. Fortunately, I had empathetic outside counsel reminding me that the deal still made sense for the extra hundred grand. And I wound up buying the building for $2.5 million.

We took more square footage than we had before, and we'll have to build out some raw space. We're going to have a higher nut. But the more professional image that the new building will project should help us win acquisition deals, which will more than cover the higher monthly payment.

If I had stayed mad about having to pay more for the building, if I had let my pride get in the way, my partners and I would have wound up losing the deal and a great opportunity. The whole thing would have been shot dead. To set my emotions aside and think of the deal in more practical terms, I needed a shot of self empathy—I had to let go of my ego for my own good, and for the good of lots of other people, too.

In the end, empathetic negotiating means leaving enough room in the deal to make it a win-win for both parties. It's a fine line: Naturally you want the best possible deal for yourself, but you've also got to preserve the right of the guy on the other end to make some profit for himself, too. Negotiators who beat up the other guy, and cut his profit margins too thin, wind up going through the muscle and hitting bone. And when there's no empathy for the other guy, whether he's a vendor or customer, you won't survive the deal. To protect yourself, leave your ego behind.

# Chapter Eight

# *The Importance of Self Empathy*

For too many years, I kicked myself for not finishing college. I always felt uncomfortable when golf course conversation would inevitably turn to the question, "So, where'd you go to school?" Instead of letting myself off the hook and accepting the path that my life had taken, I continued to regret not earning a degree and persisted in blaming what I believed were my own shortcomings.

This sense of shame would reappear whenever I was stumped by a business problem. When I first started Majestic Mortgage, for the life of me I could not comprehend my profit and loss statements. I had been an excellent math student in high school and even taken honors courses, but my difficulty with the P&L reports was not about math. It reflected a disconnection between how the accountants and I thought and communicated. They would rattle off their accountant-speak and I would nod my head as if I understood, but the truth was that I didn't know what they were talking about. They might as well have been speaking Chinese.

Today I understand that different people have different strengths. But at the time I assumed that my failure to grasp the P&L resulted from my lack of education. Or worse yet, I thought that I just wasn't smart enough.

But there was more at stake than just my self-esteem. Running my business without understanding my P&L was like flying an airplane and not knowing how to read the instruments. And sure enough, my company almost crashed. The mortgage market swings daily—interest rates rise, refinancing falls—and I have to make management corrections in flight, like whether to add or rearrange staff. But far from being nimble, I found myself sputtering behind.

I was detached from my financial statements and relying too much on my accountant. "Why should I worry about the books?" I lied to myself. "I'm paying the accountant to do it. He's the pro."

What I didn't realize at the time was that entrepreneurs and accountants think in fundamentally different ways. Their brains are wired differently. Because numbers are only one part of his juggling act, the entrepreneur tends to think in approximate figures, while the accountant, concerned exclusively with dollars and cents, is compelled to tally every last penny. Problem was, by the time they furnished my P&L statements 45 to 75 days after the month had ended, it was too late for me to make timely adjustments to my business. Worse, the 19-page reports were written in arcane accountant language that I simply could not understand.

Deep down, I knew that I couldn't let this situation continue, but it took a close brush with bankruptcy to slap me awake to the seriousness of the problem. In 1994, just before I re-branded my company with an empathy-based culture, my internal accountant misallocated a loan. He told me that it was on the pipeline when in fact the loan had already gone through. It was as if I thought I had made a deposit into a checking account when I really had not, and then I starting writing checks and paying bills with money that wasn't there. In short order, I went from thinking that I was making a little bit of profit to finding out that I had lost tens of thousands of dollars. My cash flow was nearly choked off. But I groveled with vendors and begged for their forgiveness, and somehow managed to weather this nearly catastrophic period for my company.

Even with the problem of the financial statements staring me straight in the face, I was still a long way from solving it. I continued to blame myself. Feeling that I had missed the boat on a university education, I turned to seminars instead. I spent more than

$4,000 in a vain attempt to learn how to read my P&L statements, but I still wasn't getting it. "I guess I'm just not smart enough for this," I told myself.

But now I realize the real problem was that I was not practicing The Empathy Effect for myself. Even as I tried hard to empathize with other people, I still refused to give myself a break. Consequently I was not only undermining my own best interests, but those of my employees and customers as well.

In retrospect, the problem seems obvious: The accountants were trying to teach me from an accountant's perspective—and their way of looking at things is simply not in my DNA. There's no shame in that. I should have just said, "Listen, guys, I'm a business owner, not an accountant, and you've got to translate this information for me."

Instead, my pride and embarrassment kept me silent as the accountants continued reaching into their 55-gallon drum of numbers.

I thought I had hit a wall, but the obstacle turned out to be a veiled blessing. It inspired me to look for a solution that was based on accepting my strengths and weaknesses, rather than to continue wasting my time fighting against them. Eventually I created a radically different format for my financial statements that would also give me a whole new perspective on mortgage banking—and spur faster growth and larger profits for my company.

Instead of trying to think like an accountant, which clearly wasn't going to work for me, I made my accounting department adapt to the way I think—in terms of one transaction at a time. "One Transaction Thinking," or OTT, reconnected me to my financials and transformed my business. It combines productivity reports on closed loans with my P&L, so I can accurately assess my processing costs and revenue per loan. In our sales organization, revenue comes in loan by loan; in a manufacturing company, it would arrive widget by widget. Expenses, on the other hand, come in lump sums—$18,000 for payroll, $11,000 for rent. Before I discovered OTT, whenever I would try to find a figure in my P&L, it was as if I had thrown it out, and then was having to sort through a Dumpster to try and find what I had lost. With OTT, we would keep the revenue-per-unit intact, and break down the lump-sum expenses to a per-unit cost. The system makes it easier for the entrepreneurial mind to understand numbers. With financial and productivity information blended into one report on a single, 8.5" x 11" sheet of paper, I could start making more informed management decisions. Sometimes the conclusions I find through OTT are the opposite of what a financial statement by itself would suggest. One Transaction Thinking not only revolutionized my business, but it also has become one of the most popular topics that people fly across the country to learn about in my seminars.

## Give Yourself a Break!

The story of how my failure to understand the accountants' P&L inspired me to create the simpler and more effective OTT format illustrates the importance of practicing The Empathy Effect for ourselves. I want to be clear about this: Self empathy does not mean selfishness. It couldn't. Selfishness is the polar opposite of empathy, and in its presence there can be no Empathy Effect. Self empathy is about accepting yourself, and forgiving your own mistakes and failures. It means giving yourself credit for having had the strength and the courage to try something bold in the first place, even if your efforts didn't work out exactly as you had hoped. Self empathy shows us that even so-called "failures" and "mistakes" impart valuable lessons that can lead to exciting new possibilities, many of which turn out to be bigger and more important than what we were originally attempting before running into the "failure" or the "mistake" in the first place.

Parallels to other forms of The Empathy Effect are clear: Just as the empathy wheel turns in a self-perpetuating circle, generating more and more positive results, self empathy allows us to grow—while a lack of it leaves us stuck in the mud. With self empathy, we recognize that every experience has its value, whether it was a "mistake" or just time spent in a menial job. Nothing is ever wasted. Hosing down greasy floors with scalding water in the middle of the night during high school might not have seemed to bode well for a prosperous future, but the experience taught me that extra hustle generates higher reward—and it left me with a life-long empathy for people who perform manual labor. Every experience, no matter how modest or difficult, teaches us something that we can benefit from later. I know a guy who took a job in a shopping mall bookstore after graduating from high school, for barely more than minimum wage. He worked there during the years when other kids his age were attending college and earning their degrees. The pessimists said he was wasting his time, but to the contrary, he was learning valuable lessons about customer service and how to speak professionally on the telephone—experiences that stayed with him as he later earned a bachelors degree and was hired in the public affairs department of a major corporation. Later he became a magazine writer and eventually started a successful communications-consulting business.

Just as every company has its own culture (whether those in charge realize it or not), people have their own personal cultures—mental and behavioral habits and assumptions, patterns of how we respond to others and to the world. Like business owners assessing whether they practice The Empathy Effect, we can all benefit by asking ourselves, "Is there empathy in my personal culture, for others and for myself?"

If the answer is "yes," then you're probably living a richer, happier and more fulfilling life than if the answer is "no." An absence of empathy in your personal culture leads to conflicts and bitter feelings that eat away at your health. The good news is that it's never too late to change.

## Don't Let Pride Limit Your Growth

I began to realize that to practice The Empathy Effect for myself, I had to be willing to acknowledge my missteps. Otherwise I would be obstinately refusing to let myself grow. Pride is a subculture of ego, and ego extinguishes The Empathy Effect. I couldn't let pride stop me from doing the right thing. My personal culture had to be open-minded to the idea that mistakes and failures are learning opportunities. Too often we see just the opposite—people are afraid to admit their mistakes and argue endlessly to defend themselves, getting nowhere and burning valuable energy that could have been used in a thousand productive ways instead. Refusing to accept and learn from our mistakes is a self-defeating attitude that stymies growth. As always, a lack of empathy is a dead end. Blocked from progressing forward, we end up going backwards instead. If we never stop to consider how our actions and attitudes affect other people, whether they're friends and family, customers or employees, then we have no chance of growing closer to them. Similarly, when we deny empathy to ourselves, we're more likely to regard mistakes and failures as shameful humiliations to lock away in the dark and never examine again, except through the defeating lenses of self-pity and regret. Self empathy, on the other hand, gives us the humility we need to learn and grow.

Along with pride, fear is a barrier to The Empathy Effect, and another obstacle to personal and professional growth. After wasting years punishing myself for not understanding my P&L, and then finally creating a better system that owes its very existence to that lack of understanding, I began to see that without self empathy, people become stagnant and make the same mistakes over and over again. People who have no empathy for themselves are more likely to treat the symptoms of a personal or professional problem, but never uncover its root cause and find a way to move forward.

If I had persisted in blaming myself for not understanding the accountants' P&L, instead of finally having the self empathy to accept the fact that their way of thinking is different than my own, my company might have collapsed into bankruptcy years ago. Instead of achieving success, I could have become an embittered failure—all because I wasn't practicing empathy for myself. As always, The Empathy Effect is circular, with wide, far-reaching ramifications: Not only would I have cheated myself by not practicing self empathy, but I also would have sunk my company, let down my customers and employees, and failed my family. When I think of the prosperous lives my employees have enjoyed, and the home that my wife and I have built for our children, and how easily it all could have gone down the drain, it makes me shudder.

So often, people don't pursue their dreams because they're afraid that they won't be able to forgive themselves if they fail, or if something bad results from their venture.

"I can't go for it," the person lacking in self empathy tells himself. "What if I trip, and fall flat on my face? People will laugh at me. I'll be humiliated."

Stifling your ambitions because you're worried about what other people will think only robs you of your highest potential, and leaves your dreams dead by the side of the road.

## Ignore the Defeatists!

For anyone who wants to benefit from the practice of self empathy, I offer the following advice: Never listen to people who try to discourage you. Their defeatist attitude is a panicked reaction to the threat that your ideas and ambitions pose to them, not an expression of their sincere concern for your welfare. Rather than protecting someone from failure, discouraging words actually *cause* failure. This antipathy effect smothers the promise in people, and it's a terrible shame. Architects of wasted human potential, the defeatists say your plans will never work—because they don't want you to rise to a level that's above their own. And if it so happens that your plans don't work out as you had hoped, the defeatists can hardly contain their glee.

"See! I TOLD YOU it wouldn't work!"

But they've got it wrong again, wrong as saying that Mexico is north of Minnesota and Canada is south of Texas. Practicing The Empathy Effect for yourself—and by extension, for those around you—means realizing that even when you fail, you're better off for having tried. The lessons you glean from the experience will put you that much closer to hitting a home run the next time.

Unfortunately, some people let the fear of failure, of having to face the gloating defeatists, paralyze them from even trying. If the word "fear" were an acronym, it would stand for "False Evidence Appearing Real." When your confidence is down, you're less likely to take the bold steps that could bring a tremendous reward. It's easy to see how a lack of self empathy poisons dreams and achievement. The Empathy Effect means believing in yourself enough that you don't care what the threatened defeatists will say.

Again I'm reminded of Seabiscuit: What if his owner had given up on the horse and its jockey, as he came so close to doing? Fortunately he practiced The Empathy Effect instead, allowing the horse to run and win—and to become the legend that he is today.

When you're an entrepreneur doing something bold and new, you don't always know if you're making the right decisions. The waters are uncharted. But as long as it feels right and you believe in the idea, it's best to follow your heart. In his inspirational book *The Traveler's Gift*, author Andy Andrews imagines a vast warehouse filled with all the great advances for humanity that could have become realities if only their inventors had not given up on their ideas and dreams. Maybe there would have been a cure for cancer or blindness, if only some person somewhere had pushed a little harder and believed in himself a little more. At the same time, we can consider all the breakthroughs and innovations that do exist, but might not have if their inventors had acquiesced to the discouraging words of the defeatists. Look at the Wright Brothers: People laughed and called them crazy, but the brothers weren't deterred. To the contrary, the negativity of the naysayers only strengthened the Wright Brothers' resolve, and their successful flight at Kitty Hawk changed the world. Nearly a century later, the skeptics would scoff at the idea of selling bottled water and gourmet coffee.

## Learn from Failure, Strive for Success

Although self empathy encourages us to learn and grow from our mistakes and failures, it does not diminish our drive to succeed. The Empathy Effect would dissipate like steam in the wind if someone tried to fail, thinking, "What will I get out of this?" I don't believe we can learn from our mistakes unless we've first tried our hardest to get it right. Insincerity is antithetical to The Empathy Effect, and self empathy doesn't reward laziness or short cuts.

As the realization sank in that I needed to practice The Empathy Effect for my own mistakes, I also saw that my company's culture would benefit from a similar form of self empathy. Just as I would examine my own missteps and failures to see what went wrong and how I could improve for the next time, at Majestic Mortgage we started performing the "autopsies" on problematic loan files. As a company we needed the collective mindset that accepts looking back and performing a critique, so that we could take a good lesson from a bad experience. Empathy for failure requires courage, and hiding from mistakes is a form of self-defeating cowardice.

When an occasional loan file runs into problems, it could be that the work wasn't done right, or maybe a flawed system was to blame. As an organization we need the strength to say, "We're going to look at this and find out what went wrong." Just as an individual shouldn't be afraid to confront and dissect his own mistakes, our company culture can't afford fear. No one is going to lose their job over an honest mistake. Everyone on the staff is inculcated with the idea that our organization strives hard for perfection but won't punish ourselves or one another for occasionally making mistakes. Instead, we'll embrace the lessons and perspectives that our missteps provide, to help us improve our services in the future. Performing a loan autopsy wouldn't work if the employees thought, "Oh, my God, my mistake is going to be exposed and I'll be humiliated! I won't get my raise—*or maybe I'll be fired!*"

Once we started performing the loan autopsies, the results often surprised us. In many cases, the problem that was uncovered by the autopsy would turn out to be something completely different from what we had initially expected. Examining mistakes would become a tremendous growth mechanism for us.

## The Double-Edged Sword of Loyalty

But even when employees view procedural breakdowns as opportunities for improvement and not as something to fear, as a business owner you sometimes have to face the fact that a member of your team does not belong there. You might lose someone and feel bad about it. Maybe it's a person you've developed a friendship with, but unfortunately they just don't share your core values.

For many years I had a manager who fit that description. He and I got along well and had become friends, but I finally had to accept that his personality as a boss did not fit with The Empathy Effect culture that I was trying to create at my company. He had a hot temper and was verbally abusive with the employees. The worst incidents were occurring during a period when I was doing a lot of soul searching, asking myself, "What do I want my company to look like?" I knew I didn't want it to resemble the antipathetic picture that this manager was painting, so we parted ways, and are still friends today. Sometimes being honest with yourself means admitting that certain relationships, even ones that you may have been involved with for years, are not healthy. I had a chance to be with him years later, and found that he, too, had learned from his mistakes.

## Huddling at Base Camp

When you're first starting out as an entrepreneur, you make more mistakes because you've got less to lose. You can be more aggressive, more of a riverboat gambler. One irony of self empathy is realizing that it's this very recklessness—and the mistakes it causes—that make our younger years such an important period of learning and growth. Later on, when you're older and have accrued some net worth, you naturally become less inclined to take chances because you're worried about losing what you have. Companies are often the same way: Resting comfortably at middle age on a foundation built during their daring early years, they lose the nerve to take chances. Mature companies become afraid to make mistakes, believing that they can't afford the embarrassment. A lithe young company can stumble and jump right back up again, but when an institutionalized brand slips, the organization faces public humiliation and the wrath of its shareholders. Occasional fiascoes reinforce this fear, like the introduction of the "New Coke" in the mid-1980s, or the American Medical Association's lumbering misstep in 1997 when it announced a deal to endorse Sunbeam products. (There are honest mistakes, and then there are just plain stupid ideas!)

But with self empathy, we see that the fear to make bold moves at middle age is just another barrier to reaching our highest potential, no different than the tragedy of dreams dashed by discouragement and indecision. To be fair, at middle age it does become a larger-scale endeavor to maintain an empathetic balance for all of your responsibilities—including your job or business, spouse and kids, family finances and investments, personal hobbies and interests, etc. Balancing The Empathy Effect with all of these spinning plates requires effort and will, in direct and opposite proportion to the easy path of selfishness and antipathy.

Microsoft is a great example of a company that took a huge risk after already achieving market dominance. The company's early operating system, MS-DOS, commanded more than 95% of the computer market. Giant waves of cash were crashing in, and the company was under no obvious pressure to change. Apple Computer, meanwhile, was a much smaller player with a cult following among its customers. Still, Microsoft couldn't deny that Apple's point-and-click simplicity, and its windows that popped open, was infinitely more user-friendly than the gloomy MS-DOS format, which required users to type arcane codes and formulas just to execute basic computing functions. Apple's more appealing model, from the palatable product name to its remarkable ease of use, was a classic example of an empathy-based USP improving upon a more cumbersome original. Unlike MS-DOS, which might have been admired by engineers and scientists, the Apple Macintosh operating system was designed with the needs and convenience of its users in mind. In other words, the Apple computer was designed with empathy.

Microsoft had already made its fortune, but the company saw that it wouldn't have a future unless it embraced the change that it knew was coming. Whether with a company or an individual, self empathy means setting pride aside and being honest with yourself. Conversely, shutting your mind to the truth and fighting to preserve the status quo means lying to yourself. Just like the discouraging words of the naysayers or a person's refusal to take positive lessons from his or her mistakes, denial of change is a self-defeating proposition. With the vision that's essential to The Empathy Effect, Microsoft made the bold decision to bet the company. By introducing the Windows operating system, Microsoft would render its own market-dominating MS-DOS product obsolete. It could be argued that Windows was an enhancement of the Apple model, which itself was an improvement upon Microsoft's original MS-DOS. Each new plateau in computing solved more of the users' problems and made their lives easier—The Empathy Effect defined.

After seeming to lose its way before the turn of the 21st century, Apple is red hot again with its wildly popular iPod and iTunes music systems. And what about Microsoft? Has the once-mighty innovator become bloated and stagnant with middle age, reduced to the status of an upgrade company? The days of its spectacular growth seem like a distant memory, and the company's share price has traded in a narrow range during the last several years. Has Microsoft become a lumbering dinosaur, afraid to take risks and fated to sink into the tar pits?

I don't think so. Maybe it's because as a middle-aged man with self empathy I can relate to a middle-aged organization like Microsoft, but I believe that the company is going through a temporary "base camp" period to assess its direction and determine which way the wind is blowing, before it starts climbing again. It's reasonable to think that if your organization is not moving forward, some other company will gain ground on you. But you can't be climbing all the time, because you'll wear yourself out. There's a time to climb and a time to camp, so you can plan your push to the next level. Microsoft is catching its breath, getting ready for another big burst of growth. As its history with rendering its own MS-DOS product obsolete by launching Windows makes clear, Microsoft is smart enough to embrace change rather than resist it. Just as pride and the stubborn refusal to admit a mistake can seriously damage an individual's life or career, a company that's more worried about saving face than changing with the times will suffer from its own lack of self empathy. Cash-rich Microsoft continues to plow money into research and development, and the company is working on new innovations that could bring it roaring back into favor again—with its customers and on Wall Street. In the meantime, Microsoft is still a widely held, Dow-component stock, and I believe that investors who are willing to huddle a while longer at base camp will eventually be rewarded with an ascension to the summit.

## Self Empathy and Investing

Your personal investments are in peril when you ignore your gut and let the fear of what others will think guide your decisions. If everyone is telling you that you have to do something because everyone else is doing it, then it's probably best to do the opposite. Self empathy means believing in yourself, even at the risk of being ridiculed by others. Following the crowd is never a good idea. Just as people let the bull-run hysteria of unproven tech stocks blind them to common sense in the late 1990s, some even going so far as to take out credit-card cash advances so they could hop aboard a market rise they thought would never end, after the market bubble burst many of those same people began propagating the idea that stocks in general would never again be a good place to invest. Such thinking is nonsense, of course. Rather than reflecting an honest belief that equities are bad investments, the defeatists may have just been stomping sour grapes because they lacked the self empathy to admit to themselves, let alone to others, that they had made a mistake by plowing their savings into the stocks of Internet start-up companies that had never made any profit. Rather than risking what they considered the unforgivable shame of admitting a mistake, the naysayers tenaciously clung to the idea that their depleted nest eggs were the market's fault, not their own. It's never easy to own up to our mistakes and missteps, but as with other forms of bitter medicine, we're usually better off choking it down so we can regain our health.

When I was younger, I had asked my friend and real estate-investment mentor Tom Conrardy, "How do you know when a deal is right—and more important, how do you know when it's wrong?"

"If a deal doesn't feel right," he told me, "then it's not the right deal to do."

No matter what kind of investment you make, trusting your gut is a big part of self empathy. When you go against that sixth sense, you'll probably wind up regretting it.

I'm reminded of a story that someone once told me, about a man who bought a row of dilapidated three-flats in Chicago's Lincoln Park neighborhood during the 1960s. At the time, this part of town along Clark Street was considered a slum, and everyone told the man that he was crazy to put his hard-earned money into those run-down properties. But luckily for the investor and his children, he practiced the self empathy to believe in his own instincts and ignore the naysayers. It took a very long time, but by the 1990s the Lincoln Park neighborhood had become the wealthy, yuppie haven that it is today, and those once-decrepit buildings along Clark Street are now worth many millions of dollars.

## The Cross-Generational Empathy Effect

The Lincoln Park real estate investor made his daring move when he was young and unafraid to take risks, before the doubts of middle-age might have interfered with his ambition and his belief in himself. I'm a strong advocate of people making bold moves early in their lives and careers, to gain experience and lay the foundations for their futures. But for people who've reached middle age and all the responsibilities that come with it, the humility of self empathy means being a big enough person not only to admit and grow from mistakes, and to be willing to take new risks, but also to not be threatened by the presence of young blood. The self-empathetic person or company at middle age knows that it's to everyone's benefit to have some enthusiastic young people around, whose optimism and energy help balance the staid experience and wisdom that come with the years. Young people help keep any company sharp and on the edge. This phenomenon is no different than when grandparents find their lives rejuvenated by their grandchildren, or when young parents can once again view the wonders of the world through the eyes of a child.

Actor Jeff Bridges, whom Baby Boomers remember as the fresh-faced kid in 1970s movies like *The Last Picture Show* and *Thunderbolt and Lightfoot*, now finds himself in his mid-50s, passing into the older generation of Hollywood stars. (Bridges played the damaged but determined horse owner in 2003's *Seabiscuit*.) But with the self empathy that befits such an accomplished career, Bridges said in an article in the July 2004 issue of *Interview* magazine that working with younger actors lets him "live vicariously off that freshness in their eyes. They keep you on your toes, because often... they haven't worked too much. Or even if they have, they've worked with good directors and haven't developed a lot of bad acting habits." (Bridges' comments remind me of my own experience with employees who had spent time working in antipathetic companies, and why young hires fresh out of school are often unspoiled and more amenable to the idea of an empathetic company environment.) The person interviewing Bridges, by the way, was the much younger, rising star Philip Seymour Hoffman, a character actor whose many roles have included one alongside Bridges in the movie *The Big Lebowski*. "Over my career," Bridges continued, "I've also had really great experiences working with first-time directors.... They come at filmmaking with fresh ideas."

By welcoming the presence and influence of younger artists rather than feeling threatened by them, Jeff Bridges lends The Empathy Effect to everyone involved. He benefits by feeding off their energy, and the young people learn from his experience. Perhaps the biggest winners are the people in the audience, who get to enjoy a better movie as the result of this on-screen chemistry. Compare this positive, empathetic scenario to its opposite, where an aging but egomaniacal star would resist and conflict with the younger talent. In a case like that, the virus of bad blood infects everyone involved. Resentment and recriminations breed more of the same. Jeff Bridges, on the other hand, is a perfect example of someone who can feel empathy for the younger generation because he has walked in their footsteps before himself. He started out as a young actor and remembers what it's like to be in that position. Bridges doesn't let his pride prevent him from working well with younger people or from growing as an actor as a result. In other words, Jeff Bridges practices self empathy.

## Going through Life with a Checklist

When I look back on the early days when I was first forming my empathy-based culture, I realize that I was learning what I liked through the process of eliminating that which I did not like. It was as if I were walking through life with a checklist:

"Well, that idea didn't work," I would tell myself, or, "That's not the kind of thing I want to see at my company."

Sometimes the experiences were difficult and unpleasant, and I might have felt like I was wasting my time. But now I can see that trial and error is an essential part of anyone's education.

Practicing self empathy means being willing to head down a road where the outcome or the destination is not clear until you reach it. You might discover that you don't like the conclusion, but that's okay—at least you gave it a try, and now you know not to go there again. And you wouldn't have taken that chance in the first place without the self empathy to believe in your own ideas and abilities.

## Accepting Your Own Strengths and Weaknesses...

As one of my favorite authors, John Maxwell, often advises, it's best to play to your own strengths—and to work with your limitations, not against them. Practicing self empathy means that if you can't hit a curveball, then admit it to yourself and wait for the fastball instead. As Maxwell points out, if you're a level-four at something—hitting baseballs, singing or playing the piano, to name a few examples—and you lack the natural talent to be a seven or an eight, then no trainer, coach or teacher can ever take you higher than a point or two above where you started. But that's all right, because accepting your limitations leads you to focus on your strengths instead. If I hadn't accepted that my way of thinking is different from how accountants think, I might have continued trying to force myself into a mold where I didn't fit, rather than turning my energy to the more productive path of creating my One Transaction Thinking system. Practicing The Empathy Effect also means having the humility to surround yourself with people who are strong in areas where you are not. I found that I had to recognize everyone's role without trying to pigeon-hole any-one—and to keep an open mind for new directions in which a team member or an employee might want to grow.

## ...and Those of Others Around You

It took a difficult experience for me to learn that practicing The Empathy Effect for strengths and limitations also applies to the expectations that we have for others. I had hired someone whom I really liked as a person, but I failed to recognize that he wasn't suited for the job. This individual has many strengths and abilities, but he will never be a great salesperson. He simply does not have a natural talent for sales. People like him, but he doesn't inspire the confidence that would make them feel comfortable letting him handle their $200,000 mortgage.

Later, as the company expanded, I wanted this person to grow along with it. I tried to promote him into an executive position, hoping and expecting that he would be great at it. But once again he lacked the innate talent for the job. It's not that he was a bad person or a bad employee; it was just that I had pushed him in a direction for which he was not suited. In my desire to see him grow and prosper, I had forgotten the empathy that would have allowed me to encourage his strengths and accept his weaknesses.

What I found was that as a company starts to grow, weaknesses that might have been hidden begin rising to the surface. Along with flawed systems and procedures, people's shortcomings also become more noticeable and apparent. As my company grew, I couldn't ig-nore the fact that I had assigned this person to a task that he really wasn't good at. And this lapse in my empathy would have far-reaching, negative ramifications—for me, for the company, and for the individual whom I had promoted into the wrong job. Instead of finding a position that was a good match for his skills and would foster a healthy sense of self-worth for this individual, I had pushed him into a position where no one would be more acutely aware of his weakness for the job than he would himself. Without intending to, I had hurt both of us.

I had promoted someone into the executive ranks who did not have any innate leadership skills, or even the desire to be a leader. Because leadership had always been important to me—going all the way back to my experience on the park district hockey team when I was in high school—I had wrongly assumed that other people would welcome the chance to become leaders themselves. I wanted this particular individual to pursue a management position more than he wanted it himself. In retrospect I can see that he probably went along with the idea just to please me, but he wasn't following his heart. We both could have achieved The Empathy Effect by admitting to ourselves, and to each other, that he was not the right guy for the job.

Loyalty, I learned, can be a leader's greatest asset or his worst liability. Sometimes we want to move a person up the ladder based solely on our loyalty to him or her, or on our desire to promote from within the company, even when deep down we know that the person isn't qualified for the promotion. Everyone suffers as a result: The person in the wrong job is unhappy and feels inadequate, his or her tasks are not performed properly, and other members of the staff begin to resent the situation as well. Inevitably customers will also feel the sting, as the virus bred by the mismatch starts to infect standards of service. In turn, profitability takes a hit, which raises tensions and lowers employee morale even further, and so on. The Empathy Effect is lost when the leader puts himself in the backseat, saying, "Well, this guy has been with me for so many years; let's give him one more chance, just one more chance. He'll get there someday." In a case like this, a dose of The Empathy Effect might taste like bitter medicine—everyone, including the person stuck in the wrong slot, will be better off if someone new is hired who's better suited for the position. As the empathetic leader you have to make the painful but necessary decision to either cut the underperformer loose—or ideally, laterally reassign that person to a more appropriate position that matches his or her strengths. That way, you don't stymie growth for the entire organization. The Empathy Effect dries up and blows away when personal pride or sentimental loyalty forbids you from honestly assessing the talents of others to create a powerful, empathetic and profitable organization.

When you first start out as an entrepreneur, you're discovering things as you go along. What I found was that as my company grew, I had to adapt my way of thinking to accommodate the changing situation. Otherwise, I wouldn't be able to grow. But as a business owner faced with a difficult decision, you might find that your mind is playing tricks on you.

"If I let this friend go and hire someone new from the outside, how do I know they'll be a good person? Maybe they'll rob me blind. For all of his faults, could it be that the person I already have is really the best one after all?"

I realized I would have to leave my comfort zone and make decisions that I'd never had to make before. I might have to let somebody go, despite my emotional attachment to that person. It would be better for the company, and probably for the individual as well. How many people have been fired and felt humiliated, but then later looked back and realized it was the best thing that had ever happened to their careers, because it freed them to pursue some great opportunity that provided a better match for their skills and personality, or maybe even for their dreams? It's like the man whose wife leaves him: At first he thinks it's the end of the world. Later he looks back and realizes, "Thank God she left, because otherwise I never would have met my second wife, and she's the perfect woman for me."

## The Self Empathy of Instincts

At any stage of your life or business career, practicing self empathy means trusting your instincts. In the beginning, they may be all that you have. That feeling in your gut, or that little voice in your head, can be an extremely valuable resource when you learn to heed its advice.

How many times have you ignored a gut feeling and then regretted it later? A friend of mine told me a story about walking in a hilly part of rural Connecticut on a dark, moonless summer night. He literally could not see his hand in front of his face.

"Don't take another step," the little voice told him.

Guess what happened? He took the step anyway, plunged ten feet off a cliff and wound up in the hospital with a sprained knee. Needless to say, he was lucky—ignoring his instincts could have killed him.

But when we first start out in business, we might not have confidence in our instincts because we haven't had time to develop a track record yet. Instead, we sometimes try to go by the book, whether it feels right or not. In my case, I tried to run a rate-based mortgage company at first, because judging by the formula that all of my competitors were following, that's what the book recommended. It wasn't until after I'd endured several years of operating with no profit and an uneasy sense in my gut, that I finally embraced my instincts and changed course toward an empathy-based culture, which has since made me my fortune. In the beginning I questioned my instincts. Later on, I learned to trust them.

So often for a business owner or entrepreneur, the tape is playing but nobody is listening. Your gut might be telling you that something is the right thing to do, but you don't give yourself the opportunity to hear it. Self empathy means creating a situation for yourself where you can say, "It's gut time. What are my instincts telling me to do?"

## Recharging Your Batteries

How do you give yourself the chance to listen to your instincts? Typically it won't happen when you're burned out from working all the time. I find that when I'm really stressed, I can't even make a decision about where to go for lunch. I'll get in my car and turn in one direction, and then another, and then another. When I find myself frozen with indecision about where to eat, I can only imagine the effect that my stressed-out state will have on the more important decisions I have to make. To find the opportunity to listen to my gut, to achieve that self empathy, I need to be refreshed. And that requires some time away.

Once again, racehorses provide a good analogy. For a working horse, life can become a mundane, daily grind. Oftentimes you'll get your best results from a racehorse after taking her out of training and letting her relax on a farm for a couple of months. The horse is free to run around all she wants, and she doesn't have to be at the track at six o'clock in the morning when the feed arrives for all of the other horses. On the farm she can graze at her leisure. This time off refreshes the horse's mind and body, so she can come back stronger than before.

With people, the burned out workaholic starts to make bad decisions. Or worse yet, he makes no decisions at all, because he's stuck on the treadmill of his daily scramble. When you're first starting out, maybe you've got eight or 10 employees and you're the salesperson extraordinaire—the typical entrepreneur career path. At that stage, you're running and gunning, and have little choice but to be a workaholic. Of course, you're also young and full of physical and mental energy. But as time passes and you need to become more of a strategist to grow the company, you also have to start taking more time to recharge your batteries, especially the mental ones. Self empathy means recognizing your need to refresh, to know when you're no longer thinking clearly and it's time for a break. Maybe little things are starting to bother you, and you don't even realize that you're burned out.

You can't send a racehorse to the farm for just a few days—she needs at least a month. Similarly, most entrepreneurs don't take enough time off to refresh themselves, especially at the beginning. They'll say, "I won't work this weekend." But you can get so wrapped up in your business that it might take a week or 10 days to sufficiently detach, so that you can find the perspective to answer important questions like, "Is this really what I want to do with my company? Am I taking it in the right direction? Is my vision still intact? What do I need to rethink, and retool?"

Just as a racehorse requires the wide-open spaces, I personally have to get away from the office to an entirely different environment so I can rest and recharge. I'm a much better performer when I return after taking three or four days off every $2^1/_2$ weeks. My executive team calls it my "$2^1/_2$-Week Rule." Twice a year, I'll take a cruise or go to Hawaii for a few weeks, and just zone out and not take things too seriously. The workaholic crowd might accuse me of overindulgence (if not downright laziness), but self empathy means ignoring the pressure to conform and doing what you know is best for yourself—and by extension, for your company, staff, customers, family, etc.

## Working "On" the Business

Part of the reason that some entrepreneurs fail to grow their companies is that they spend all of their time working *in* the business, rather than *on* the business. Working in the business means you're down in the trenches, ducking whizzing bullets and bursting bombs, doing the day-to-day work of managing your staff and providing your product or service to your customers. Don't misunderstand me: Working in the business is important. In fact it's essential, especially at first. But eventually you've got to step back and look at the business with a wider lens.

Working *on* the business is the key to growth. In his book, *The E-Myth: Why Most Small Businesses Don't Work and What to Do About It*, author Michael Gerber describes "the tyranny of routine" that saps the creative juices from so many workaholic entrepreneurs. He recounts the story of how the McDonald brothers, founders of the eponymous restaurant, couldn't grow their business because they were too busy flipping burgers, scooping fries and ringing up sales at the cash register. They never took the time to step back from the daily grind and see the business from a broader perspective. It wasn't until Ray Kroc came along and bought them out that the brothers' brilliant fast food concept began to expand, eventually growing into the world-renowned mega-brand that it is today. Kroc was selling milkshake mixers when he met the McDonalds, and as an outsider he was able to view their business from a fresh perspective. By working on the business rather than in it, he hit upon the idea to franchise the McDonald's concept to other owner/operators. Growth was stratospheric, and before long the company became a household name.

Several years ago, I retained the services of a professional business coach named Daniel Harkavy. He has a program called "Building Champions." Harkavy taught me the importance of "on" time.

"Here's what I want you to do," he said. "The first Friday of every month, get out of the office for the entire day, and spend that time working *on* your business, rather than in your business."

At first I was a little bit skeptical. How could I work on my business if I were out of the office?

"You've got to be in a different zone," Harkavy said. "Go to a library, a coffee shop or a bookstore, someplace where you can detach completely from the environment of your office."

At the time, I was struggling to figure out how to improve my company's profit-sharing program. At first, we split profits evenly, according to salary. Everybody earning a certain annual salary would receive the same bonus. But it didn't take long for me to realize that the system wasn't fair. Two employees sitting next to each other might both have been earning $35,000 a year, but one of them had a much stronger work ethic than the other and consistently showed stronger results. I felt bad about it, but I didn't know how to make the profit-sharing program more equitable.

Following Harkavy's advice, I determined to spend the first Friday of the next month away from the office, so I could focus exclusively on trying to solve my profit-sharing problem. I got into my car and drove. I didn't even turn on the radio, but just drove and drove. Finally, about 45 minutes later, I pulled into the parking lot of the Grand Geneva resort, in Lake Geneva, Wisconsin. The resort has a sprawling lobby overlooking an outdoor swimming pool, and there's a loft area on the second floor.

Upstairs it was quiet and there was nobody around. At first, I really struggled over the quandary of how to improve the profit-sharing program. I sat in an overstuffed chair with my laptop computer, but for the first couple of hours I didn't do a thing. I just sat and stared. "This is stupid," I said to myself.

But I had made a commitment that I would spend an entire nine-hour day working on this project, and I was determined to see it through. And then, all of a sudden, the creativity started to flow. By the end of the afternoon I walked down from that loft with a plan to completely overhaul my company's profit-sharing program, using a peer-voting system that assigns a rating to each employee. The size of the bonus check is tied to that rating. To this day, the solution that I devised during that first afternoon of "on" time remains unchanged, and it has helped foster employee loyalty and satisfaction at Majestic Mortgage, as well as spurring higher profits.

Finding a way to improve my company's profit-sharing program was a major project for me, and one that at times I had doubted my ability to accomplish. I credit Daniel Harkavy with coaching me through it. The experience taught me that the mind works in mysterious ways—you've got to give it the chance to flourish in the right environment, which is why getting out of the office is so important. Staying cooped up does not allow for the new experiences that provide fresh ideas and perspectives. Ever since that day at the Grand Geneva, I have continued to schedule on-time—initially just on the first Friday of each month, but now I do it almost every Friday. In retrospect I realize that had I tried this approach earlier in my career, I might have grown and progressed at a much faster pace. But at the beginning I would have felt guilty about being absent from the office for even one Friday a month. In our work-obsessed American culture, we're taught that stepping back from the grind is something we should feel ashamed about. In many companies, even leaving the office for an hour-long lunch is frowned upon, and the fact that the break actually makes people more productive is hidden in denial. When I first started taking "on" time, I had to overcome the guilt of leaving the office for the day. This was a big change for me, since I had always thought that I needed to be the first person to arrive at the office in the morning, and the last one to leave at night.

But what I realize now is that "on" time is a form of self empathy. As always, self empathy means being honest with yourself—while its opposite, self denial, undermines your best interests. Toeing the workaholic line and never leaving the office not only would have stymied the creativity I needed to discover some of my best ideas, holding back my personal potential, but it also would have prevented me from creating a more empathetic environment for my company and employees. Although it might be the opposite of what the mainstream would dictate, taking time away—whether to work on the business or just to rest and recharge the batteries—has been essential to my success as an entrepreneur.

Self empathy means knowing your own rhythms. Are you a morning person or a night person? Different people are creative at different times. There's no shame in having your own unique patterns. It pays to be honest enough with yourself to recognize when and how you perform at your best.

Of course, an empathetic leader who acknowledges his or her own cycles also has to extend that understanding and flexibility to the rest of the management team. I've tried to sanction the idea that no one at my company should become burnt out. The other executives also have the freedom to follow their own rhythms and take "on" time, or just time to refresh themselves. As salespeople, they are entrepreneurs within my company. I don't necessarily recommend extending this flexibility to the rank-and-file; without tenure at the company, they might try to abuse the privilege.

Like most businesses, mine is somewhat seasonal, with spring and fall the busiest home-buying seasons. Sometimes we need to bust it out and work 10 hours a day, six days a week—but not all the time. No one could keep up that speed every week, every month, every quarter. At some point, the pace has to slow down for everyone.

"Get your rest now while we're in a lull, because later on when the busy time jumps into high gear, I'm going to need you at your best."

When employees hear an understanding attitude coming from the leader, The Empathy Effect is in full play. The leader's empathy for himself extends to his awareness that others need the same opportunity to recharge, and in this empathetic environment a sense of mutual gratitude is created.

## Don't Be Afraid to Look outside Your Own Industry

Just as ego dissolves The Empathy Effect and pride blocks self empathy, narrow-minded thinking is a barrier to growth. I'm not necessarily referring to the refusal to consider new ideas or points of view, although such an attitude would definitely be narrow-minded. For entrepreneurial business owners, even those with generally open minds, the problem is that sometimes it simply doesn't occur to them to look outside their own industries for ideas on how to grow their businesses. In my case, if I had worn blinders and searched only within the mortgage industry for solutions to my business problems, I might never have found them.

Around the same time that I made the conscious decision to rebrand my company with empathy-based USPs, I also took a hugely important step by joining the Young Presidents Organization (YPO). New members have to be 40 or younger, with a president or CEO title, and have a certain minimum number of employees and level of sales revenue.

Self empathy means not being too proud to ask others for advice. Through my meetings with YPO, I've learned valuable lessons and perspectives from business people in industries other than my own. Regardless of your particular business—whether it's selling home loans or gourmet sandwiches, like Jimmy John's—there are always common denominators. We all deal with issues involving customers, employees and profitability. The YPO forums consist of 10 to 14 business owners who are not in the same industry. In fact, it's a YPO rule that there cannot be people from the same industry within the same forum. Since they don't have to worry about giving away their secrets to a competitor, the participants are more willing to share ideas and information. Everyone in the forums knows they're safe to say whatever is on their minds. While many business owners stagnate because they only look for answers within their own companies or industries, the YPO members can bounce ideas off successful presidents from a wide variety of industries, with complete confidentiality in an intimate, non-threatening group setting. And many of them go on to achieve greatness.

When presented with examples and ideas from other industries, our brains seem to absorb lessons and information more readily than when we only look internally. People tend to cast more doubt on advice that comes from within their own industry, because they think they know everything that there is to know about their own field. "Well, that concept won't work in *my* company," someone might say, waving their hand dismissively. Sometimes we know too much about our businesses for our own good, and it creates a kind of narrow-minded myopia. On the other hand, if an idea comes from an industry in which we've never worked, we might be more receptive to it. I can honestly say that I've learned most of my business acumen from people outside of my own industry—both through YPO and from all of the business books that I have read over the years.

Automobile baron Henry Ford provided a great example of how an entrepreneur can grow by having the self empathy to look for new ideas outside of his own industry. Although the man and his brand are often considered pioneers in the automobile industry, Ford did not have the first car company. There were some 2,000 others operating at the time that Ford entered the business in the early 20th century. But manufacturing processes were too slow and costly for the other automobile companies to grow.

It was during a visit to a meat packing plant in Chicago that Ford got his first look at an assembly line. He watched with fascination as the cow carcasses were systematically taken apart, piece by piece. With the vision and belief in himself that comes with self empathy, Ford realized that he could use a similar process to build cars, but in reverse: Just as the meat packers disassembled animals in a methodical progression, Ford would use the assembly line to manufacture his cars, piece by piece. The vastly improved efficiency of this process would dramatically speed up production time while also slashing costs, allowing Ford to offer his cars to the masses at an affordable price and thus dominate his industry. To this day, the Ford brand remains a household name, thanks to the fact that its founder was not too proud to look for solutions outside of his own industry. He had practiced the self empathy to acknowledge the strengths and limitations of his original business model, rather than stubbornly fighting against them. As a result, Ford opened his mind to an idea that changed his life, his company, the automobile industry and the world. That's the power of The Empathy Effect.

# *Mission Accomplished*

Now that you've finished reading this book, I want to tell you how important it was for me personally to finish creating it, with the great help of my writer, Greg Beaubien. Completing *The Empathy Effect* might be one of the hardest things I've done so far. But looking back it's clear that the process of writing the book was itself an example of The Empathy Effect. As a speaker my knack is to make complex things simple, and my life experiences form the basis for the book. Greg's talent is to write. With empathy for each other, we accomplished our goal of finishing this book. In fact, I think we might have even found a new way to write a book. For more information, visit TheEmpathyEffect.com.

*Tom Ward*
*The Majestic Group*
*847.970.4261*